HIRING TALENTED TEAM PLAYERS
A Guide to Getting it Right

HIRING TALENTED TEAM PLAYERS
A Guide to Getting it Right

Kingsley J. Wimbush

Smashwords Edition

Published on Smashwords by:
Fletcher F. Wimbush
Wimbush & Associates, Inc.
519 Cherry St.
Brea, CA 92821
Phone: 719-637-8495
E-mail: Info@TheHireTalent.com

Hiring Talented Team Players: A Guide to Getting It Right
Copyright 1994, 1995, 1996, 1999, 2000, 2003, 2006, 2007 by Kingsley J. Wimbush

All rights reserved. Without limiting the rights under copyright reserved above, no part of this publication may be reproduced, stored in or introduced into a retrieval system, or transmitted, in any form, or by any means (electronic, mechanical, photocopying, recording, or otherwise) without the prior written permission of both the copyright owner and the above publisher of this book.

Smashwords Edition License Notes
This ebook is licensed for your personal use only. This ebook may not be re-sold or given away to other people. If you would like to share this book with another person, please purchase an additional copy for each person you share it with. If you are reading this book and did not purchase it, or it was not purchased for your use only, then you should return to Smashwords.com and purchase your own copy. Thank you for respecting the author's work.

ISBN: 1539010406
ISBN 13: 9781539010401

Table of Contents

Foreword · vii

Chapter 1   The Hiring Game · 1
Chapter 2   Attitude · 16
Chapter 3   The Four Basic Pegs and the Many Holes · · · · · · · · · · · · · 36
Chapter 4   What Does the Ideal Candidate for the Job Look Like? · · · · · 55
Chapter 5   Finding Profitable Candidates · 71
Chapter 6   Effectively Screening Resumes · 85
Chapter 7   Questions for Your First Phone Contact · · · · · · · · · · · · · · 94
Chapter 8   An Effective System to Handle the Paperwork · · · · · · · · · · 98
Chapter 9   The Key Stumbling Blocks to
                 Good Interviewing—Exposed · · · · · · · · · · · · · · · · · · · 102
Chapter 10   Getting the Truth · 122
Chapter 11   Interview Questions · 132
Chapter 12   Reference Checks · 159
Chapter 13   Legal Issues · 170
Chapter 14   Testing · 182
Chapter 15   Improving Your Competence In Hiring · · · · · · · · · · · · · · · 188

About the Author · 191

Foreword
by Fletcher Wimbush

The publication of this book is in memory of the author, Kingsley John Wimbush, born in Perth, Australia on Dec 5th 1945, and who passed in Colorado Springs, CO on March 10th 2013. For my father there is no better way to honor him than to continue his work and promote the values he studied his entire life. Kingsley was born to discover the truths about life, the universe and everything else.

From an early age he showed his entrepreneurial spirit. He started by raising rabbits for local pet stores. Early in his adulthood, he began a successful handyman service; this is where he began to learn about marketing and management. Later in life, he became a successful consultant for leaders throughout the business world. He developed a dynamic set of assessment tools that are still being implemented by companies who desire to achieve lasting success in their businesses. As he progressed through his professional career, he found it necessary to teach himself how to do everything, whether he self-taught himself proper grammar or how to write HTML code; he would be unrelenting in his search for knowledge. Like many of us, he navigated his way through faith and finding deeper meaning in life. Early on, he found and joined the Church of Scientology where he became a successful mission holder. This success was not without a price; one thing he never learned was politics. His success scared other leaders within the organization which lead to his excommunication in 1982. Nevertheless, he continued his efforts to help others discover themselves and become better people. He eventually found Christianity which changed his perspective on self-enlightenment. Christianity helped him rediscover the underlining principle that drives all social behavior: the self versus the other. Early on, he found focusing on other people's needs, wants, and desires produced better outcomes in our personal and professional lives. There have been many books written on this subject whether they are management, sales, or self-improvement studies that are all based on the common link between the individual and their ability to identify and serve the needs of others. With this in mind, we move forward, exploring how to build teams based on this "Golden Rule" we find in every religion and text on spiritual enlightenment.

This book is a guide to understanding how to select people who are both good natured and possess the talents needed to be successful in the business world. Many of these ideas have helped me personally achieve insights into others, allowing me to become a productive leader and person. I owe much of my personal and professional success to my father. Throughout my life he was my friend, coach, mentor and teacher, he was always there for me without judgment. From an early age he instilled in me the importance of always learning and growing as a person, that quest never ends for us still here. The process of self-reflection, humility and enlightenment are qualities he taught me to respect and practice. By releasing this publication, I hope others may enjoy his insights and follow Kingsley's drive to self-empowerment through the service of others.

Hiring the best people is not one sided. It serves both the person joining a strong team and the team itself. When a team is dynamic and formed with great consideration towards inspiring excellence, everyone wins. When team members are highly engaged, they think clearer, follow leadership with conviction, are more creative, and achieve previously unattainable goals. This is a rewarding experience for everyone involved. Ultimately, it is our customers and clients who receive the most amount of value from developing dynamic teams. As you read through this book, please keep in mind that at the end of the day, the work you put into building your team is for the direct benefit of those you serve.

Chapter 1

The Hiring Game

The most common hiring mistakes *seldom* come from selecting unqualified people. As the saying goes, "Hire for skills; fire for attitude." The biggest mistakes come from hiring attitude problems and personality misfits. This failure is easy to understand. Very little is published on exactly how to detect attitudes during interviewing. And personality is too complicated to determine from interview questions.

Twenty seven years ago when I first set out coaching business leaders, they all seemed to want to focus on one subject—the frustrations they had with a handful of their problem employees. Yet, they liked them during the interviews and honeymoon periods but then became frustrated with them for the following reasons:

* Being emotionally unstable, moody or defensive.
* Having hidden agendas that neglected what management wanted.
* Upsetting customers with an indifferent attitude.
* Neglecting responsibilities.
* Personality clashes or stubbornness.
* Often absent.
* Going through the motions only to save their jobs.
* Lazy.
* Continuing to break the rules even after being confronted about it.

This is what I discovered. I started by asking my clients why they didn't address the symptoms. I remember Russell Borghese (made up name) looked at me in silence trying to figure out a good way to sugar coat his explanation or switch the subject. Then he told me about all the sleep he had lost over a particular troublemaker and how he hoped circumstances would magically improve. When I suggested he confront this employee, he said, "Yes, that's a good idea." Unfortunately, despite the compliment—nothing happened. The idea of confronting negativity, even though he knew he should, was at the very bottom of his mental priority list. In addition, the idea of firing problem employees was met with a "You've got to be kidding" look.

At first, I thought they didn't know how to manage their employees. But, when I encouraged them to coach, train or confront their troublesome employees, the return on investment was minimal. When these employees quit, were laid off or fired, my clients were always relieved. The truth was they had hired the wrong people. In addition, unless a major lay off occurred or someone prodded them, the hiring mistakes became part of the scenery.

When I delved into the situation of difficult employees, it never turned out to be a qualification problem. If you have managed for a while, I bet you know what I am going to say the problem was. Yes, these people had attitude or personality problems.

Amazingly, most problem employees are great when they start. They must know how to fly under the radar. It seems as if the employer and employee go on a honeymoon. The good news is that some leave after a couple of weeks—but with truck loads of blame.

I concluded that the most difficult employees had attitude problems or had the wrong personality for the job they were doing. I heard very little about those who were unqualified or lacked education. My clients were either doing a good job at screening out those types or they noticed the incompetence and booted them out quickly. I should also note that some employees with low emotional intelligence (EQ) were not doing their fair share.

Why, Why, Why?

Why were these problem employees so effective at making it through the mine field of interviews and getting the job? I observed several reasons for this.

Sometimes clients would advertise for candidates. When the resumes came in, they were able to eliminate many of the unqualified. However, to my amazement, after the interviewing and reference checks were over, about 80% (my guess) of the "qualified" people had negative or inappropriate traits. If we were lucky, we would find one good candidate from an ad that ran two weeks on multiple job boards. So sorting through the masses of unemployed only took one minor hiccup, and another problem was invited to the team. Unfortunately, there was only a very small percentage of productive good-natured people looking for jobs. And an even lower percentage had the right personality for the job.

Also, most managers had never gone to "interviewing school." Their candidates on the other hand were street smart, savvy, and well trained in the hiring game. These applicants usually had a history of being fired (under the heading of laid off and other palatable reasons). With all the experience going from interview to interview, reading books, attending job connection groups and attending seminars, they learned how to con most interviewers. A problem employee is *not* dumb; in fact, most of them are the smartest people you will ever meet (seriously).

In hindsight, the biggest reason for hiring problems was a failure to understand the telltale indicators for these types. Most of my clients knew the indicator of how often they go to greener pastures and how often they get fired. But, if that was not obvious, they erroneously thought that those who acted nicely and were likeable in an interview would also be that way on the job.

I think you will agree the loyal, hard-working, good-natured types seldom quit their jobs. These people seldom get much of a chance to practice interviewing skills. This makes interviewing even more confusing because the best can look the worst and the worst can look the best!

The Big Picture

Throughout twenty-seven years of closely examining hundreds of organizations, I have witnessed the result of corporate America's inability to sort the good-natured people from the problem types by just looking at the people they have working for them. Based on what clients have told me and what I have personally witnessed, I diagramed these percentages:

* Five percent are good-natured employees who are hard working, loyal, cooperative, positive, thoughtful and competent. These employees need little or no supervision. Unfortunately, they are often taken for granted.
* Thirty percent are mostly good natured and hard working but have some minor rough edges.
* Thirty percent have personality rough edges, such as rule breaking, personal agendas, outspoken negativity and stubbornness. Their rough edges are easily managed, and their productivity more than makes up for the irritations they cause.
* Thirty percent have a poor attitude. They are sometimes unwilling, offensive, unmanageable, absent and selfish (have their own agendas), but are productive. Their faults can be hidden for up to a year. While half of them respond satisfactorily to discipline and need plenty of it, the other half keep relapsing back into bad attitudes. The ones that relapse are similar to the next category, but not as bad.
* Five percent are the quintessential problem employees. They are unmanageable, emotionally unstable, offensive, and they scheme away on their own agenda—yet can they do a bang-up job. They often show an unyielding what's-in-it-for-me attitude. They don't (and won't) respond to correction, discipline, punishment, fines or anything else you can dream up. They may pretend improvement for a few weeks. This is why the "three strikes and you're out" law came into effect for criminals—these types don't ever get it. No matter how hard anyone tries to change them, they won't. And, just like the previous category, the extent of their negativity can be camouflaged for

up to a year after being hired. In reality, most problem people could care less about hiding their ugly side after the probation period is over and they have their medical benefits. Employers keep them around because they are often the most skilled, but the hardest to confront and the most secretive about the total number of problems they cause. Don't get me wrong, employers know about the problems, but not the overall extent (at least until the employee leaves).

Most managers are relieved when one of these types are gone. The co-workers who had to work closely with them are also relieved. The manager may feel sorry about the loss of skill, ability and know how, but overall she is also relieved.

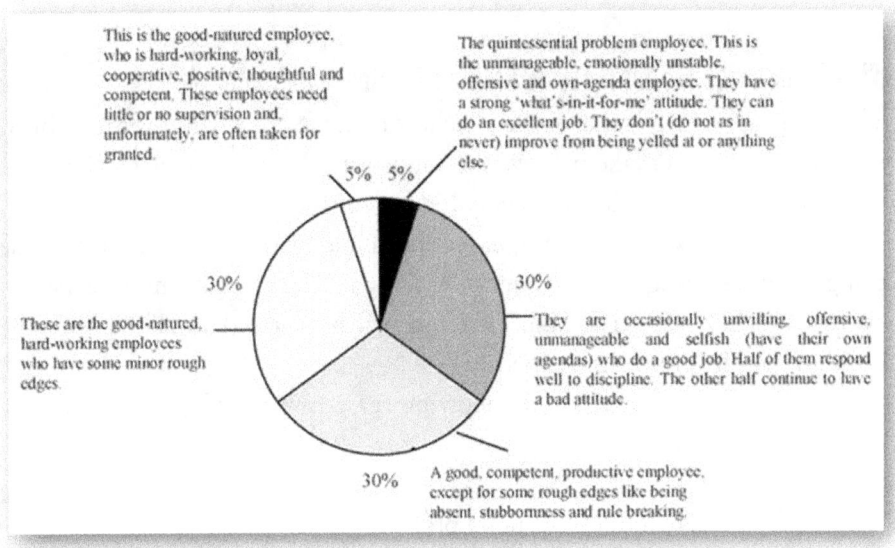

Many problem people, who are hired but detected early on and let go, are not part of this pie chart. However, they are part of the hiring mistakes.

Isn't it amazing that companies can survive? And, do you know what—many small ones don't. From many studies of new companies, I have heard that only about 5% survive their first ten years. I'm sure you have noticed some big ones failing, but many of the ones that don't make it are quite small. They are picked off one by one, not because of market conditions (their competitors survive), but poor management. Because the success of companies depends on people—no, the right people. One of the biggest reasons these failed companies are pushing up daisies is due to management incompetence when making hiring decisions.

A good exercise is to think about those who report to you, by putting them in the pie chart. Be honest. Now you know if your hiring process is better or worse than the average by looking at your own company's pie chart. If you don't have people reporting to you, the pie chart won't be as real, unless you are very observant. The brutal, horrible, painful truth is that too many problem employees, personality misfits and those with low emotional intelligence get hired.

What is the Price Tag for Ignoring Problem Employee Indicators?

Those on the top right side of the pie chart rarely make a net profit for a business. Sure they will make money, but not profits. As any manager knows, the full extent of their damage is usually hidden until they leave.

The overall cost of a bad hire, I have been told by those who research these things, can be as high as two times the annual salary of the employee, especially when they are entrenched. Therefore, the higher and more highbrow the position is—the greater the expense.

If you examine some of the following reasons, you will understand why the cost is so high:

* They make money but not a profit.
* They cause the team unnecessary stress.
* They upset customers with missed deadlines and indifferent attitudes.
* They wreck everyone's day as well as team spirit. (They scare some.)
* They cause good workers to be falsely blamed.
* The time, money, and effort to train them must be spent again with a new replacement.
* The price for typical learning mistakes needs to be paid for once again.

* The manager is under continuous pressure to weigh the pros and cons of keeping them. (Stress.)
* The manager has the unpleasant task of confronting them. Or, the manager who won't confront them has an unpleasant feeling from, avoiding, feeling guilty, and avoiding some more, until the inevitable blows up.
* The manager has the rotten task of firing them.
* The manager may have to live with guilt, due to the fired person's family situation.
* Lost productivity from not having someone who is the right fit for the position
* Costs related to recruiting a replacement.
* Frivolous unemployment claims or unfounded litigation for falsely perceived employer violations of the local job codes.

For example, one client hired a very energetic salesperson who bothered the other sales people and lowered the overall sales (even though his numbers looked good), and when he finally got the boot, he had already brainwashed a good employee into quitting. His boss caught him taking the best leads for himself in a sneaky way. The financial loss, from lost sales, the expense of replacing him and the one he negatively influenced, easily exceeded two times his annual earnings.

Another walking disaster was a desktop publishing wiz, who repeatedly chose to ignore job priorities. He also refused to recheck details, which caused customer complaints. His failures caused many headaches and slowdowns among the team. His manager's manager finally figured out who was causing the trouble and allowed the manager to give him his walking papers. The bill for the company's hiring blunder was at least twice his annual salary. This manager concluded—skill alone was of little value without cooperation.

The emotional suffering and stress for keeping a problem is even higher. A supervisor is either faced with the unpleasant task of continually disciplining the person or letting the cancer drift to others. If you add the hard cash and personal grief from hiring a person like this, the value of hiring good people becomes a matter of survival.

My management consultant brother once told me that all his clients who had problem employees in key positions were in financial trouble. The moment they corrected the matter, their businesses did well again. This is serious business.

Understanding the Solution

You can compare interviewing to dating, especially after a divorce. The person is concerned the new date may also be a problem. But the person is nice and loving during the mating ritual—the same way the problem person was. Subtle inquires produce all the right responses. But, because of the past lousy experience, there is uncertainty. Who can blame the person for that? On the other hand, the new love may really be great. You just don't know.

At this point, you are probably wondering the same thing I did twenty seven years ago. If you can't tell problem people from their outward manner, then how can you tell— especially when they seemed to have been on previous jobs for a long time? So, I decided to figure out what other hiring pros had written. Amazingly, they only touched on attitude and focused more on the art of interviewing.

The main hiring principle in my head was that past behavior was the best predictor of future behavior. This worked well for skills and competence but not for detecting attitudes. It seemed that almost all candidates were convincingly honest, loyal, hard working and cooperative. In other words, the questions available at that time were not cutting through the act and revealing the truth.

For many years, I suggested to my clients to closely question the reasons candidates gave for leaving previous jobs, which did help. But, few job applicants "had ever been fired." They were laid off and quit for bigger challenges but, surprisingly, never fired (I'm sure you know how that works). Another strategy was to refuse to hire anyone who had worked for more than three companies in five years. Both ideas helped a little, but I really needed interview questions to expose the problems from the good-natured people.

Then, one day in 1991 when I was studying honesty testing, I made a life altering realization. Let me explain. Honesty tests are made up of statements related indirectly to honesty principles. These assessments ask for opinions in such a way that right or wrong answers are difficult to determine by someone who lacks basic honesty principles. The key was asking for opinions, N-O-T past behavior. After massaging the idea for a while, this is what I discovered:

IN ORDER TO EXPOSE ATTITUDE TRAITS YOU MUST ASK A PERSON ABOUT THEIR CORE VALUES, WITHOUT TIPPING YOUR HAND.

In other words, ask for the person's opinions about honesty, loyalty, supportiveness, responsibility and so on. But, do it in a way the job seeker has *no clue* what you think are the right answers. This is easier said than done. Thankfully, later in this book, you can learn this method of questioning along with the interview questions.

Let me give you an example. Ms Interviewer asks Mr. Job seeker, "What would you do if your boss asked you to lie about a delivery date?" (Job seeker wonders what the right answer might be, but the interviewer hasn't indicated anything.) So, falling back on his core values blurts out, "I would do what my boss wanted. If he asked me to lie, I would lie. If he didn't want me to lie, then I wouldn't." (By the way, some people actually answer the question that way.) The interviewer ends the interview and sends him on his way, saving the company from another problem.

After I had figured out the formula for attitude interview questions, they started to flow like a creek after a big storm. Then I applied these questions every time I interviewed someone. I wrote down the answers I got to the new questions for future research. After about 6 months, I researched how they had worked in reality. And sure enough! My clients indicated improvements through this type of interviewing. Then through many years of trial and error and with the help of my clients, these questions have been refined. They are organized in their entirety in Chapter Eleven.

The Attitude Test

At the time of the realization, I had been upgrading my business-personality assessment. So, with my new insights and my focus on testing, I wanted to take the next step and also develop an assessment that would detect the problem types.

I knew how honesty tests were put together, so all I needed to do was change the subject to attitude traits. Although my clients did have the occasional problems with theft of money and equipment, the far more common problems were attitude ones. So, I developed a new attitude and integrity assessment at the same time I worked on the interviewing questions.

Years later, I found out that other Test Publishers had also come up with attitude assessments. I continue to improve mine based on client feedback—also officially known as "Predictive Validity" (how well does the assessment do what it is supposed to do by checking back about a year later). The last version 14 was released in 2012 and has a 90% accuracy rating. My clients must be happy with this assessment as they vote with their dollars year after year.

An attitude and integrity assessment shows different degrees of attitude tendencies similar to the pie chart mentioned earlier. If the client wants to confirm the results, all she has to do is ask the prepared questions organized in Chapter 11—especially in the areas the assessment indicated possible problems. When you add interview questions, reference checks along with an attitude and integrity assessment, you will slam the door shut on any new problem employees entering your workforce. Also, this assessment will save those precious hours of interview time.

I notice my clients who use this assessment have also changed their work environments. They no longer tolerate paying for enemy like activities. They seem more upbeat, profitable and are much more able to withstand economic turndowns.

Although my clients voted dishonesty, personal agendas, absenteeism and emotional outbursts as big problems, I also realized some of those same problems were coming from personality selections. In other words, they were hiring personality types that didn't fit the jobs. In lay person's language, they were trying to fit round pegs in square holes.

Personalities

Identifying personality profiles is most important for job fitting, but it is also important to uncover traits that are dangerously weak or too compulsive.

Because interviewing for personality traits and profiles is almost impossible, this is a case where I strongly recommend using a personality assessment before making a hiring decision. I also developed one of these, which I explain in Chapter 3.

Personality is a *big* hiring subject. It is also important when dealing with people. When you read Chapter 3, it will translate the relevant personality features a supervisor needs to know into plain English. I also included the interview questions concerned with personality in the chapter that deals with interviewing techniques, Chapter 11.

Common Interview Mistakes

These are the four most common blunders interviewers make:

* Talking too much. (Explaining, not interviewing.)
* Emotionally believing the candidate is perfect before digging deeper.
* Jumping to conclusions from scraps of information.
* Carelessly divulging to the candidate what the interviewer hopes to hear.

A full explanation and cure for these are covered in the two interviewing Chapters 9 and 10. After some careful study, the full extent of these bad habits will become obvious. Once you see what you're doing, your ability to interview will improve and continue to improve. And, if you interview with the questions suggested in Chapter 11, you will seldom make these mistakes. Those questions force you to ask about values and present situations, without exposing what you hope to hear. You will also find out more than just scraps of information.

Covering All the Bases

Before you hire someone, you should answer the 12 queries below:

1. Does the candidate have all the skills to do the work?
2. Does the candidate have the education to do the work?
3. Does the candidate have the experience to do the work?
4. Is the candidate bright enough, quick enough and creative enough?
5. Will the candidate be satisfied with the amount of money and benefits the company can afford to pay?
6. Does the candidate have a good nature (Hard worker, positive, responsible, truthful, loyal and emotionally stable? Not a problem or criminal?).
7. Will the candidate fit into the culture of the company?
8. Does the candidate have the right personality for the work?
9. Does the candidate have the interest in doing the work?
10. Does the candidate like working inside (desk jockey) or outside?
11. Will the candidate be able to meet the company's attendance requirements?
12. Does the candidate have the ability to perform specific job functions, with or without special accommodation? (See Americans with Disabilities Act in the chapter on legal questioning).

You can make this your check off list before making an offer to a candidate. When clients ask me if they should hire someone, I just go through the list and determine what queries haven't been answered. Then I suggest they explore those unknown or doubtful ones. Some ask me to interview the person checking 6 through 9 when they are not sure. Checking all these twelve queries is another insurance policy to prevent the waste and problems of hiring a wrong person.

Query number 7: will the candidate fit the culture of the company? Focuses on whether or not the person and the company have similar core values. One thing I have found over the years is that if the employer has good moral values, then a person with a good attitude will usually fit in that culture. You must have good moral values or you wouldn't be reading this. So, all you need to do is make sure your job seeker doesn't have a poor attitude and you have covered queries 6 and the most important parts of 7 in one fell swoop.

If you are like most managers, you are probably buried under mountains of papers and fighting fires on several fronts (some of them set by your own problem employees). The idea of going through all twelve queries must be frustrating. Thankfully, there is an answer to the time-crunch squeeze.

The Good News

If you look at the twelve queries just covered, you will notice that the first five are usually easy to find out about. And any improvement will increase your hiring accuracy and save yourself a bunch of time messing with the unqualifieds. One obvious time saver is to quit talking so much. Also, better interview questions will get to the meat of the matter faster.

If you decide to use personality and attitude assessments, you will eliminate time on queries 6, 7, 8 and some of 9 (interest in the work). I say some of 9 because the right personality for the task is almost another way of saying interest in the task. You will quickly figure out number 10 (likes working inside or outside), number 11 (attendance) and a few remaining questions about number 7 (cultural fit) with a few questions. If you know your legal way around hiring (see Chapter 13 on legal), number 12 will seldom come up as a problem. With the time saved, you will be able to scrutinize more applicants to find better people.

If you don't like the idea of using the Attitude Assessment for number 6 and 7, then you can become an expert by studying the next chapter. That chapter makes the obscured integrity and attitude indicators so obvious that even the most polished, problem candidates will be easy to recognize. Never again will you be fooled by the friendly, personable cheese-eating grins.

Personality assessments are another story. It is very time consuming and almost impossible to interview for personality profiles. You either measure the candidate's personality or cross your fingers and hope queries number 8 and 9 will be right. Chapter 3 describes in street language the highlights of personalities. It teaches how to translate personality assessment results into hiring decisions. And, yes, if you decide to figure out a person's temperament from the interviews, that chapter will help.

Other Advantages

Think about your competitors missing the tell-tale signs of a problem employee and personality round pegs in square holes. You on the other hand, will now recognize and pick the productive good-natured candidates from among the sea of those looking for jobs. Your competitors may end up with the problems and will spend their time and money psychoanalyzing, arguing with, worrying about and counseling them. Your business becomes more and more successful; you and your team will have more fun.

When you start interviewing for attitude traits, you will recognize more and more of those types already on board. Your tolerance for their behavior will diminish considerably, and your understanding of their cost will increase. You may even feel more motivated to confront and fire them.

What About the Scarcity of Good Candidates?

I was hoping I didn't bring that up. The biggest challenge in hiring is finding good candidates to interview. I know you know this and that is why I wrote Chapter Five. It costs money to find good candidates, especially using recruiters. In order to make a commitment to invest in finding good candidates, you will want to feel confident about those hiring decisions. If you can identify truly good people, you can afford the cost of lining up good candidates.

On the subject of recruiters, they mostly focus on experience, skills and education, which is valuable. Don't tell them to weed out the attitude problems or mess with personality. They are rarely trained to do it, so wouldn't know how, and not motivated to reduce their commissions. In addition, you sure don't want them coaching their job seekers to practice cheese-eating grins. It is up to you (not them) to be vigilant on those attitude and personality traits.

Where to Go from Here

Looking for the right person can wear a manager down. Interview exhaustion is real. It causes managers to short cut requirements to reduce the number of interviews. It's therefore important to work out a good hiring procedure that produces great employees, before the interviewer gets exhausted. This book is written for the purpose of helping you establish such a process.

The next two chapters examine attitude and personality. Chapters 4 through 12 are in the sequence of actions to hire effectively. You can study those chapters just before the action needed to help really implement the ideas.

The best strategy for the war on negativity requires Guerrilla tactics. Study this book. Apply what you learn. Make adjustments and keep on applying. Use attitude and personality assessments before making hiring decisions. Hire the right people. Save your company from the cancer of negativity, mediocrity, and misfits.

Chapter 2

Attitude

The people with the worst attitudes can easily talk their way past many interviewers, get the job, keep the extent of their negativity hidden and remain employed too long. This is because most interviewers don't realize what it takes to uncover the attitude. In fact, it is a rare manager who can detect it, although there are many who think they can. The way to detect attitude is very different from finding out about qualifications.

What are Attitudes?

In the first chapter, I referred to the person with the worst attitude as a wolf and the person with the best attitude as a good-natured person. The most basic description of attitude has to do with a willingness to support the boss and the team. The willing have good attitudes; the unwilling are wolves. Or, the good attitude types have the long-term benefits of the company at heart, and the wolves have their personal short-term greed as their goal. There are two basic types: The unselfish and the selfish.

Have you ever tried to get another employee to do something for you when it was part of her job (yes, in her job description)? Some did it willingly (good attitude) and some would conveniently forget or even protest doing it (bad attitude). We all know what it feels like to run into the wall of unwillingness.

I understand this is not a pleasant subject for many people. We like to think of everyone as good. The reality is that some really don't care what they put us through. In spite of their meanness, I personally feel they should be forgiven and helped—but not hired.

In chapter one, the twelve queries you need to answer in order to hire the right person are described; attitude is number six. I know you know attitude is important, but like many of my clients, they hadn't really thought about it enough to use it to their advantage. Many thought of it as hiring a quality person as though that was going to be obvious. Once they faced the outcome of some of the people they had hired, the picture became a lot clearer. Whatever method they were using didn't work.

Attitude is completely different from personality traits, skills and ability. For example, a salesperson may have the right personality, skill and ability to sell like gangbusters, but at the same time is a pathological liar (attitude problem). Some may think they still want her to sell until they find out she lies about forecasts, lies to customers about delivery dates, lies to production about what the customer needs and so on. Attitude can sink the ship and often does.

The best way for me to describe attitudes is by starting with the worst cases—the wolves.

Who are These Stinkers?

The wolf has many names.

* Bad Apple
* Problem Generator (my brother's name for them)
* Predators (a psychologist's name for them)
* Bully
* Troublemaker
* Furry Animal

My management-consultant brother calls them problem generators because they seem to cause unsolvable problems. For example, the boss pleads, "Could you work overtime tonight to help get this customer's product delivered on time?" "No," says the problem generator as he walks away pretending to be deaf. They sure keep employers worried, frustrated and awake at night.

Through the years of coaching business leaders, I heard many sad stories caused by wolves. Here are some of them:

* A supervisor who did the bare minimum and lied to cover her back when deliveries didn't make it on time.
* A guy who sexually harassed a coworker even after warnings were issued.
* A woodworker who would get so upset he threw tools around the shop.
* A saleswoman who took so many short cuts in explaining things to customers and writing down requirements that most of her orders ran at a loss.
* A customer service lady who would pester her boss for more pay increases and would let the phone ring too many times before picking up.
* A union leader who stirred up so much trouble that management finally ended up paying him $25,000.00 to quit.

I bet you have seen many of the same things yourself and get the picture. To complete the list would take a thick book.

The psychologist I heard talking about these types referred to them as predators. The main theme of his talk was that these people were criminals who were smart enough to keep themselves out of jail where they belonged.

The best example for you of a wolf will be the person who caused you the most problems in your life (not an ex or parent). It will be a person you disconnected from and by doing so caused the most relief. The biggest wolf I had to deal with was a business partner who spent a lot of time in bars—he should've been behind bars. He took money out of the business without my knowledge and spent it on himself. "Legal theft," I found out, is not a crime, or is it?

Here is a List of Common Wolf Traits:

* Creates unsolvable problems.
* Focuses on, "What's in it for me."
* Sees more negative than positive.
* Is defensive.
* Blames others.
* Gets into conflicts with others.
* Tries to make others feel guilty.
* Uses anger or shades of it inappropriately.
* Refuses to change.

One of the unique aspects about wolves is their competence. Look at some of the famous ones in history like Hitler, Stalin and Osama Bin Laden. They were competent in many ways. Then there are con artists who are clever enough to fool people. Sometimes they are hired and kept on board because they are so good at their job, despite their obnoxious behavior. It is also that ability to think on their feet that enables them to get jobs and fly under the radar long enough to make firing difficult.

Many clients have asked me how their wolves would affect their businesses, and no matter what I knew, I was never able to predict the damage they caused. All I knew was the result wasn't going to be pleasant.

How is the Team Affected?

I will never forget a client coming in one day and telling me how his right hand man had gone awry on him. He had previously always spoken very highly about him, but now he was a loser. Wow! As I listened to the sad story, I realized that his manager was supervising a construction job for a customer who fit the description of a wolf. One rule I had learned about wolves is that they can cause good people to make mistakes. I told my client about this and as soon as the job was over his man would be okay again—and he was. Anyone in the presence of a wolf will make mistakes. I know—I nearly got fired from a client over a misunderstanding caused by one! Fortunately, she was fired a couple of weeks later when the owner got some serious complaints about her from some of his favorite customers.

One of the places the wolf causes problems occurs in group meetings. They are the ones who sit with their arms folded making snide comments and rolling their eyes. The speaker is affected, which causes the meeting to lack the enthusiastic energy needed to motivate even the most willing.

How Come They are Still on the Team?

The biggest reason managers allow wolves to stay is the fact that they are good at their job. The problems they cause are seldom noticed by those who can fire them. Those who do notice the problems are afraid to say anything. The wolf can be compared to an iceberg; only ten percent is visible, which makes ninety percent invisible. Just like the iceberg that sank the Titanic, it was the invisible part that cost all those lives. The manager also knows that a wolf will not take kindly to confrontation so leaves well enough alone. The cost and effort to replace them is also overwhelming. So with only ten percent of the problem showing, why do anything? Action to remove usually occurs when the ten percent grows as the wolf gets braver and braver and shows his fangs.

Based on the wolf's ability to worm his way into an organization and produce, he may last for several years before getting the boot. The damage caused during that time in terms or money and stress will be considerable, yet it will be obvious only toward the end of his stay.

As a consultant, I specialize in coaching managers to deal with their wolves. Because one of the characteristics of a wolf is an unwillingness to change, I have become an expert teaching the most effective ways of taming them. The result is usually a parting of the ways. Therefore, prevention, by good hiring strategies, is the better strategy.

The Wolf can easily be detected during the Interview
Detecting wolves depends on two things:

* The skill in detecting core values.
* The ability to recognize attitude indicators.

Core Values: As covered already, the way to detect attitude is by interviewing for core values. The best way is giving the candidate made up scenarios that require decisions based on values (found in Chapter Eleven on interview questions). Unless you are lucky, you will not detect attitudes based on past behavior. This occurs when candidates explain how they felt about previous supervisors. Either way, you will need to know the attitude indicators when they surface.

Recognizing attitude indicators: If you are serious about seeing attitude indicators in an interview, you will need to be able to separate attitude indicators from other types of indicators. Because there are an infinite number of indicators, learning the few attitude ones is definitely the best plan. The good news is that the main attitude indicators are few in number.

By using the attitude interview questions in Chapter Eleven you are almost home. If you really want to make things easier, use my opinion survey on those applicants who look good after the first interview. The results will tell you how good or poor an applicant's attitude is. With both good interview questions and my opinion survey—you are almost there. Then, when you learn the following attitude indicators, you will be there. It will then be up to you to make informed hiring decisions.

The Attitude Indicators
If you look ahead, you will see a wall of print describing these indicators. Yes, it's a pain to have to know about them. No, you can't just skip over them if you want to hire talented team players. Once you learn them, you will find them a useful tool for understanding existing employees, people in your personal life and how to sort out the best people to hire.

An easy way to understand these indicators is to know both the positive and the negatives of each attitude trait. So, stripped to its briefs, the common denominator of a good attitude is a genuine, unselfish support of others. The common denominator of a poor attitude is the "what's in it for me right now" and "no one else matters." These attitude indicators are broken down into the following basic categories:

Supportive Versus Non Supportive

The major indicator of attitude is supportiveness or cooperativeness toward the team effort and the team leader. Supportiveness is the willingness to follow a leader's intentions or cooperate with another. Most wolves (bad attitudes employees) believe it's not necessary to support a satisfactory manager. They overtly, or sometimes subtly, demonstrate their lack of support especially once the job honeymoon stage is over (1month to a year). Wolves want to do things their own way. Supportive people, on the other hand, are never offended when asked to do something extra or do something outside their job description. Supportive people are willing to go the extra mile and stay late without complaining.

One way to detect an unsupportive attitude in an employment interview is to note how applicants refer to their past supervisors. If the applicant says mostly good things about eighty percent or more of his past supervisors, that is a plus. If the applicant has many petty complaints or really harsh complaints about previous supervisors, this applicant will most likely turn out to be unsupportive—and sometimes a wolf.

In some cases, the people have slaved under a tyrant. The good attitude people will be more positive, more understanding and less critical of them than poor attitude types. I'm sure you want me to tell you more specifically how they will do this. Unfortunately, there are no truly black and white answers, and there may be extenuating circumstances, but, with practice, you will learn the difference.

The best way to detect supportiveness is to give the applicant difficult, hypothetical situations and ask her what she would do. Listen for cooperation or lack of it, especially with supervisors. For example, suggest a situation where a company doing poorly financially during a bad economic time asks the employees to take a ten percent pay cut. Ask the applicant how she would negotiate to get a better deal than this, (she doesn't know if you're concerned about negotiation or what) and listen for her degree of cooperativeness and supportiveness of authority.

Many questions on the wolf test examine supportiveness because it is one of the best indicators of attitude.

Thinking of others versus "What's in it for me?"

Another sign of a poor attitude is the "what's in it for me?" approach to life. In existing employees, this negative trait shows up when they make an extra effort (not just a usual effort, but an extra effort) to be paid for every minute that is due them. They are the type to nag their supervisor for employment evaluations to get pay raises. The "what's in it for me?" employees also want more paid time off, interesting jobs, better equipment and extra benefits regardless of their productivity.

The "what's in it for me?" attitude shows up in hiring when an applicant pays more attention to benefits compared to other applicants applying for the same job. For example, asking early on about pay or how many benefits the job offers (this is a subtle indicator, but can be a very useful one). Because certain professions are made up of people more money hungry than others, you need to compare similar types. For example, a commissioned salesperson will ask about percentages within the first few sentences where most administrative assistants may not ask until the second interview. Therefore, if a salesperson and an administrative assistant both ask about money after thirty minutes, it is more likely the salesperson has a good attitude and the administrative assistant has a poor attitude. This is not a foolproof way of telling because some types of jobs have minimum pay levels, and in those jobs it is customary to ask about pay upfront. It depends more on where the applicant focuses.

The "what's in it for me?" focus can show up in other areas. One of those could be a refusal to do certain job functions. For example, "I don't do windows." It could also be a demand to have something like a corner office or new desk when the person's experience doesn't warrant such things.

Candidates with good attitudes usually don't ask about pay until the end of the last interview. They are willing to do functions that are not so glamorous as well. Good attitude people are easy to negotiate with as they trust their new employer to reward them fairly for their productivity. I don't suggest you ask about these things, but you should listen for them.

Unless the candidate has a tremendous focus on money, I wouldn't only count that as one red flag – not a reason to turn the person down.

Hard Worker versus Lazy Worker

Lazy employees work too much on the wrong areas, such as surfing the internet, chatting about their personal life at work or on the phone. The lazy types will leave before their shift is over or exactly when their shift is over ("clock watchers"), even when important work still needs to be done. For example, lazy inside salespeople whose jobs are to answer the phone and take orders might leave their desks, even when customers are on hold and it's not break time, or they may not double check their work after completing it. They won't go the extra mile and will do things begrudgingly.

Hard workers usually have a history of taking action to get things done. When their manager indicates a chore needs to be done, they do it without procrastination. Some hard workers will work more than 40 hours per week. During the course of most interviewing, the hard workers will usually bring up that they are comfortable working overtime. You don't want a workaholic because working smart is better than working hard, but a typical hard worker will put in the hours. A hard worker is an indication of good attitude.

The best way to detect laziness is to give applicants a difficult, hypothetical situation and ask them what they would do. Tell the applicant, "You have been at work all day for a company that doesn't have a late shift, but the customer's job you have been working on needs to be completed that night. Your boss hasn't said anything to you either way. The only commitment you have for that night is going to dinner with your spouse. What would you do and why would you do that?" If the person says, "It depends." (That's already a negative.) Find out what they are thinking because therein lies one of their values.

Positive versus Negative

Refuse to hire people you know are very critical. Critical people have trouble understanding the good and will spread the bad. They want to immediately change aspects of your company or how you do things. All employees will disagree with their boss from time to time, and you should consider that normal, but it's how and when the employee disagrees that indicates attitude. For example, an employee who repeatedly takes her complaints to anyone who will listen is an indication of a critical attitude. The positive (you could also replace this word with respectful) employee would make tactful suggestions directly to her supervisor. You can detect critical job applicants by how they speak about their past supervisors and the world in general, or by how easily they get bored. Any real negative statement about a boss, such as, "She was a real jerk" almost always indicates the person is too negative to hire.

Positive people seem to have only good things to say about eighty percent of past employers and are able to get along well with almost everyone. Even when applicants like this had problems with past bosses or peers over philosophical differences, they still worked hard to get along. When these good attitude people do have a criticism, it's usually specific. For example, "My boss would tend to micromanage me when I would fill out reports," not, "My boss was stupid!" There are many questions on the Wolf test that detect this exceedingly critical attitude. (In case you were wondering, these indicators are very similar to the supporter verses not supportive.)

Responsible Versus Blame

Blamers believe the problems they are experiencing are caused by someone else or something else. This attitude makes them irresponsible because they don't believe they can fix things they can. Even when you try to point out how they can fix a problem, they'll get upset with you for being unreasonable and mean.

People who truly see that they're responsible for everything that happens to them (with the exception of God) have a great attitude. Truly responsible people realize that if customers or bosses are upset with them, they are likely to have had roles in those situations. A good manager would feel responsible for a customer's job that keeps getting messed up in their department. The truly responsible will get to the root cause and do something to prevent it from happening again. They don't cry, blame, or get defensive when a risk they took goes bad. People with good attitudes will respond to blame type situations by saying they cause their own success and problems. People with poor attitudes will try to convince you that their problems or other people's problems can't be helped – and they can sound very convincing.

The best way to detect this trait through interviewing is to present applicants with blame-type situations. For example, ask the candidate if he thinks it is fair to hold a manager responsible for a late delivery if the subcontractor was late. (The examples should conceal what you are looking for.) If he says the manager is still responsible, then that shows that he tends to be responsible. Attitude is about beliefs, so asking about why he answered the way he did will be beneficial. But, I repeat, you must not indicate in the slightest way what you are hoping to hear. In fact, sound like you favor the wrong answer. For example, when he answers, follow up with a question like this, "Why would it be fair to ask a manager to be responsible for something he can't control?" Now if he tells you how the manager is still responsible, you have a responsible one.

Detecting the blame trait is often the biggest challenge in an interview because everyone blames to some degree. You have to listen carefully for indicators of this trait because they are very subtle. Testing for blame on the opinion survey is the most efficient way to uncover it.

Open Versus Defensive

Being defensive is another way of displaying blame. Defensiveness is the effort to over-rationalize, justify or deny a perceived personal attack. Defensiveness is the response of taking something personally—that is not personal—or the inability to be objective about a situation. The defense is usually immediate, unprofessional and emotional.

A candidate can become defensive when asked how she handled a problem on a job. Although she might not show how upset she is by covering it up with a smile or pleasant demeanor, you may feel uncomfortable. You can detect defensiveness most easily, if it exists, by observing the candidate's reactions.

An open person may *sound* weak by admitting faults—but he is not. I once went through hundreds of interviews that I had done looking at the answers to the question, "What are your weaknesses or areas you could improve?" I did this by reading my notes alongside this question. Not one of the answers I was given turned out to be a significant problem in any way. Therefore, if the candidate admits he or she could have been more responsible in certain situations – it doesn't mean anything! In reality, a good modest response is not an indicator of a problem.

Honest Versus Dishonest

Highly dishonest people, even though they are competent, can't be relied upon and are therefore of little value. All applicants, if asked, will say they are honest. To get around this, you should give the applicants situations that put them between a rock and a hard place and see how they respond. Give them situations where the boss's intentions are in conflict with honesty. Or, give them situations where feelings could be hurt if the truth is told, where being honest might cause embarrassment, or where decisions between greed and honesty need to made. Always follow up with questions that will expose their true (not sociably acceptable) beliefs about dishonesty.

For example, tell them that a lie about a delivery date will get a sale and then ask them what they think about that. Hopefully, the applicants won't realize what you want to hear. If they say it is not good to lie and we must get the sale, but don't answer the question, ask the question again. If they say they would lie for the sale, you know the person is dishonest. On the other hand, if they say they wouldn't lie, you still don't know for sure. So follow up with, "But don't we need to get sales to stay in business?" (This makes it easier for the dishonest to admit it is Okay to lie.) Truly honest people (rare) won't lie even if it means losing the sale. You will need to compare candidate answers for the same position. Attitude is about beliefs, so continuing to ask about their ideas is valuable. A good attitude assessment would address this subject.

Befriending Negativity vs. Confronting Negativity
Befriending Negativity is an attitude flaw, best described as too much sympathy toward negativity. People with this flaw don't believe that confrontation of negativity is good for the group or the future of the company. Managers with this fault allow the negative person to disrupt all the good people. Although this trait is more destructive in a manager, it can cause problems in others, as well. For example, a salesperson rapidly agreeing to unreasonable customer demands (doesn't bother to negotiate a compromise) can be very damaging to production, profitability and good will. These over-sympathetic people eventually feel used and walked on, which wreak their motivation and cause them to give notice or be given notice.

A person who confronts the negative could be misunderstood as being mean. Rather it is a brave person who is willing to take a person to task on his offensive behavior. So, those syrupy, nice people can have bad attitudes just like the more outspoken ones. The opposite type, who indiscriminately confronts people, is just as bad as the one who befriends negativity.

Interviewing experienced supervisors about what they would do with top producers, who are negative, will show just how friendly those supervisors are. The real "friendly" supervisor would seldom fire the negative person, even after repeated discussions with the negative person over specific negativity. Asking supervisors how many people they have personally fired gives another indication of this overfriendly trait, but you would also need to know how many employees they've managed and over what length of time.

Loyal Versus Disloyal

Loyalty is like support, but in a different way. If employees are loyal, they will stay and support their supervisor, company and leader through thick and thin. Disloyal employees are concerned about their immediate gratification and if that should falter, they'll leave for "greener pastures." This is why people who move from employer to employer, especially more than five times in ten years, usually lack loyalty and have poor attitudes. There are some situations, though, where more than five times in ten years is acceptable, such as unstable lines of work, the existence of medical problems and so on.

When you ask about why they left their jobs, you may hear several attitude indicators. Your focus should be on the disloyal type answers. For example, if you hear the reason for leaving was for a little more money or other minor benefit, you can put that down as a disloyal type indicator. In our culture, leaving for a little more money is so accepted you may not realize there is anything wrong with it. But there is. Leaving for a lot more money makes more sense, and that would not be an attitude indicator.

Principled Versus Stubbornness

People who argue and won't give in, despite good reason, may be too stubborn. Those who stick to their principles, as long as they align with the goals of leadership, are an asset. During an interview, you often have to separate stubborn from principled to detect this attitude indicator.

You can ask the applicants if they stick to their principles and when they say "yes," find examples in their past where they did this. They will either give you situations involving principles or show you how stubborn they can get. Or it will show you how trivial the arguments were or how often they argued. One hiring interviewer reported that a candidate said, "I would or would not support my boss's request for a personal favor depending on how I was asked." This applicant, later in the interview, boasted about his strong tendencies toward stubbornness. When a person boasts about a bad trait, the interview should be over.

As you read these descriptions of good attitudes, you may start thinking they are "yes" people. Actually a "yes" person is just as useless as a wolf but for completely different reasons. The ideal person would hold strongly to his or her principles.

Patience vs. Impatience
The person who is extremely impatient *and* has little empathy (it must be both) for others is a problem. The highly intelligent are more likely to be impatient than those with average or lower intelligence. Many excellent executives with good attitudes are impatient, but they are also empathetic. If the empathy level is high, the impatience usually won't cause problems. Personality testing is about the only way to discover candidates with these traits.

Long Fuse vs. Temper
Those with tempers are similar to the low patience and highly critical types. The importance of this trait rests in how bad the temper got and how often. If the person threw an object across the workspace, this is too destructive, even if it only happened once.

This is a trait that applicants will rarely admit to, and references will avoid it for fear of legal consequences. The best indicator of this trait will be problems they've had getting along with past supervisors, not being able to get along with people and speaking of others in negative ways.

This attitude indicator is not worth interviewing for directly. But, if in the course of interviewing, a candidate mentions something along these lines, you should note it.

On Time vs. Late
People who are always late usually have a bad attitude; lateness is also a sign of other negativity. When a person shows up late for an interview, even with an excuse, it could indicate the person has a bad attitude. When the candidate

shows up late for the next interview, this person is even more likely to have a poor attitude. The later the person shows up, the worse the attitude, unless there was a misunderstanding of the appointment time.

People are on their best behavior during the interview process. You'll never see them act better when they come to work. Therefore, lateness in the interview process means they'll be even later when they come to work.

When Personality Traits Become Attitude Problems

When a personality trait is extreme, it is no longer a personality trait but an attitude issue. For example, when assertiveness gets too strong, it becomes aggressiveness. When a weak trait is really weak, it too can become an attitude problem. For example, when a person is completely unwilling to listen, that is an attitude issue. These types of attitude problems are not common, but they do show up now and then.

The best way to detect an extreme trait is through personality assessments. Because people are on their best behavior during an interview, they are not likely to expose their extreme traits during one. If you suspect an extreme trait, use the questions for the trait you suspect in Chapter Ten on Getting the Truth.

Adding up the Score

A good attitude person may show some of the above negative indicators, but a person with a bad attitude will show a lot more. The bad attitude person may even have some great positives, like being extremely loyal. There are two ways of telling an attitude problem in the interview process. One is finding a situation which clearly shows the person has an attitude problem (boasts about a bad trait they have), and the other is by exhibiting more negative than positive indicators.

Probably the most difficult task is to add up all the pluses and minuses and decide how good or bad a candidate's attitude is. A good attitude assessment works in much the same way; it adds the number of times a person answers in the negative; too many negatives indicate a bad attitude and very few negatives indicate a good attitude. Compare results to other applicants until you get a sense of what is a little or a lot.

I suggest you jot down good and bad attitude statements during the interview but don't bother with middle of the road statements. You only need to note the gist of what you hear. After the interview is over, go over your notes and count the positives and the negatives. Put the attitude pluses on one side of the paper and the attitude negatives on the other, and only put attitude indicators on this paper. In this way, you can see more easily the difference between the good and the bad.

I know what I am about to tell you is not very scientific, but write down what your opinion of the person's attitude is with 10 being the highest and 0 being the lowest. If you have interviewed for attitude well, you should have a good idea out of 10 what the person's attitude rating is.

What do Helicopters Have to do with the Price of Tea in China?

Before I tell you about Helicopters, I need to tell you about the relationship between attitude and competence. So, what exactly is competence? It is made up of the following:

* Ideal personality traits for the task
* Talent
* Flair
* Ability to learn
* Education
* Experience
* Skill
* Ability to get things done
* Awareness
* Alertness
* Ability to communicate
* Friendliness

* Quickness
* General intelligence

The real value of an employee is a balance between good competence and good attitude. The balance is like the relationship between the helicopter's rotor blades. The main rotor blade is the helicopter's competence, and the small blade at the back is the attitude. If the small blade can't steady the helicopter, no matter how powerful the main rotor blade is, the helicopter is useless or even destructive. A helicopter pilot wouldn't say, "The power of the main rotor blade is the strongest I know of, and that makes up for the fact that the small rotor blade speeds up on its own sometimes." No, they are two different things and both should at least work. This is the same for competence and attitude in a candidate. For example, a powerful leader type with a bad attitude could unionize your business quicker than you could blink. If they were incompetent, they couldn't get anything done so they wouldn't be a problem. Don't be afraid of a person's power; just make sure the person has a good attitude too.

A good employee is not only productive, but also contributes to group's overall production as well. Therefore, you must have both a high competence and a good attitude to have a super employee. You can determine how valuable an employee is by multiplying the employee's attitude by her competence.

In order to do the multiplication, all you need to do is establish a rating for both attitude and competency separately. Consider the employee's attitude and give it a rating out of ten (ten being the highest). Then you would rate the person's competence again with ten being the highest. With the numbers out of ten for both attitude and competence, you can now multiply them together. For example, a prima donna may rate nine out of ten for competence, but only two out of ten for attitude. Multiplying nine by two is eighteen, which indicates this employee is usually not worth the trouble he causes. By doing it this way, the low number for a broken rotor blade multiplied by the good strong rotor blade indicates the helicopter is not good enough to use.

An employee with six for competence multiplied by five for attitude equals thirty, which is much higher than eighteen and a much more valuable employee. If you added (as opposed to multiplied) the numbers together for both this person and the prima donna, the number would be eleven for each one, but most employers would agree the six competence and the five attitude person would be a much better employee than the nine and two employee. The nine attitude and two competence person, known as the "yes" person, is just as bad as the prima donna. Multiplying attitude by competence will give you a more accurate picture of whom you should hire, whom you should lay off, and a more accurate predictor of future performance.

As a rule, when you do multiply attitude times competence, a total of twenty-five or less is an indication of an unmanageable employee or an incompetent one. Thirty would be the minimum score; and even then, you would only hire someone like that in a tight labor market. The higher the number above thirty the more profitable that employee will be.

There are obvious exceptions to this theory, such as a famous movie star that is very popular and makes the movie profitable. In such cases, a supervisor must be skilled at handling the attitude and patient with the crap. But, these cases are much more the exception than the rule. Even talented sports figures with poor attitudes sometimes have marginal value for their team or their sport. With salary caps these days, the owners may do better spending their money on more balanced players.

There is another reason the competence times attitude formula is very helpful: It forces an employer to look at both the attitude and competence and their combined value. The formula assists an employer from swaying too much to competence or to attitude by keeping them both in clear view.

Now after all that, let's look at what we need to do in an interview. I suggest you jot down both good and bad observations of a candidate when you interview. After it is over, make up two lists of pros and cons. Yes, two lists one page for attitude and one for competency. It is important you keep the pros and cons for attitude separate from the competency page. If you don't, you could have something like this. Knowledge of many software programs (competency plus) canceling out pathological liar (attitude minus). It would be like buying a helicopter when the salesperson says it is the most powerful one on the market, but the small blade stops working sometimes. One positive doesn't nullify the negative one, and they are both independent subjects and both must be good. Need I say more?

When is a Wolf not a Wolf?

Just because a woman is angry at someone does not make her a wolf. Sometimes in divorce situations the ex thinks the other is a wolf, but in reality neither are. Sometimes business partners who are having problems with each other think the same thing. Again, in most of these cases it is merely a personal upset. Don't confuse the two.

Congratulations

You will never look at candidates the same again if you made it through these first two chapters. Congratulations. Now keep studying the attitude indicators repeatedly until you notice them easily. The subject of attitudes is simple once you get it; it will make you a lot of money and save you a lot of stress – in exchange for a little study.

Personality

People may look as though they have attitude problems, when they have the wrong personality for the job they are doing. For example, you ask a shy person to call complete strangers, and you may run into a wall of unwillingness. That is not an attitude problem; it is a personality problem which is covered in the next chapter.

Just as attitude is a new and different subject to most people, so is personality. Learning the subject of matching personalities to jobs will also make a powerful difference.

Chapter 3

• • •

The Four Basic Pegs and the Many Holes

Having the right personality for an activity is like swimming downstream. For example, if you hire extroverts to sell, you will make money without much effort. On the other hand, having an expressive personality engineer, which is the wrong personality for a job, is like battling upstream. The most common mistakes are hiring people to swim across the current or giving people jobs that don't quite fit their personalities.

Personalities

First, what are personalities? A personality is made up of a mix of traits. Each trait describes an inner drive, such as Assertiveness. A trait is not a skill – it is a comfort zone, an interest, a drive. Personality is similar to gravity. Both are invisible. Both are powerful forces. Fortunately, an average supervisor can easily learn the practical use of personalities.

Therefore, if you hire people to do jobs that are outside their comfort zones, interests or drives, how can you expect them to work effectively? How can they immerse themselves fully into their jobs? If their personality doesn't quite fit the task, they won't enjoy the processes associated with the job duty. Most new employees will push through their discomfort in the beginning, just to have a job, but eventually the infatuation will wear off.

A common statement I hear from my new clients goes something like this, "The old supervisor had no backbone. He wouldn't stand up to his employees. We don't want someone like that again." Then I find out they promoted him because he was great as an individual contributor. By the way, the problem with supervisory positions usually comes down to weak communication and assertive traits.

I remember one client who hired an accounts payable person. In her department, everyone had to be a cashier in case too many customers all wanted to pay at once (why don't I have this problem?). This person loved doing the paperwork but had a problem communicating with people. When the cashier windows became busy, she would drag herself to the counter. Sometimes she would pretend the customers weren't there. Her introverted trait caused problems when the already busy cashiers had to nag her to help. They, in turn, would complain to the office manager, who had the horrible task of confronting her. The office manager's hiring mistake came back to bite and bite often because no one would fire an accounts payable person just because she was introverted.

Most people think that trying to fit square pegs in round holes only occurs with those hired for sales. And yes, sales people had better have the right personality or their days are numbered. But, every position in the organization has an ideal personality description. Let's take someone doing an administrative function that requires accuracy. If this person doesn't have much patience with detail work, both customers and coworkers are going to suffer—and so will the bottom line.

Just because a person's education is in one field, does not mean they will do well in it. This belief has cost corporations a lot of money.

The Education Myth

How many people do you know who hate their job? Too many, right? Even highly paid professionals don't like their jobs. One of the reasons (and main one) goes back to their college days when they chose a major that was not in sync with their personality. It may have been pressure from a parent. It may have been a desire to get into an up and coming field to make more money. It may have been some interesting courses. Seldom does the student study her own personality and connect it to a major. That is a skill in itself. How could an eighteen year old even know about it, let alone be skilled at it?

One day a client sent me a gal for some coaching. She worked in the accounting office dealing with numbers all day. That takes a specific type of personality to enjoy. But this gal had more of a sales personality, which couldn't be more contradictory for the job. Why then was she qualified to be working in accounting? During the Iran shake up and the Shah of Iran leaving, her dad sent her to America to learn a reliable trade – accounting. She was smart enough and graduated college with an accounting degree. Her first few jobs where in accounting, where she gained experience. But in the end, she found it difficult to buckle down and do her work. My client had to eventually let her go.

This example was an obvious mistake. In reality, most mistakes start by going to school to study subjects that don't quite fit. Specifically, a typical mistake is someone going to college to study business when they should have studied in the communications area. These people graduate and get good paying jobs in the area they studied and then acquire experience in those fields. Therefore, future employers want to hire them in the area of their education and experience yet end up with someone not quite right for the job.

As an employer, you may end up interviewing many of these ill-advised programmed people. They will have the education, skill and experience—but not the drive because they don't particularly enjoy performing the tasks related to the job.

Extreme Traits

Up to now, I have pointed out personality profiles applications. But, another great opportunity opens up when you start reading the personality crystal ball. Individual traits that are extremely weak or compulsive can indicate attitude trouble ahead. Knowing this, you will be able to cut off trouble before it has a chance to start.

An extreme trait is one that is so weak that the person is terrified to act or so compulsive that he doesn't know when to stop. A client had a bookkeeper who was so shy that whenever she ran into a problem she wouldn't say anything. After training her on the Peachtree accounting software, she would just sit there and do nothing whenever she got stuck. One day my, client's employees almost lynched him because she had run into a problem with payroll and was afraid to ask for help. After a lot of training and frustration, my client finally let her go. Most bookkeepers are not expected to be assertive, but when they are as scared as a wild cat, they can be a problem in any position.

A Great Strength can be a Great Weakness

Have you ever met someone who talks and talks, never stopping to listen? I knew someone like this who was one of the best public speakers I have ever known. I had the opportunity to go to lunch with him, but I couldn't get a word in edgewise. He had a great strength in talking but a great weakness in listening. So our strengths can sometimes be our biggest downfalls.

One day, a client called me and asked if I would interview someone. I had tested this person as having an extremely high self-confidence trait. I had warned my client that the great strength in self-confidence could indicate a great weakness in arrogance. But he really wanted this guy and hoped that somehow my personality assessment had missed the boat. I did interview him and wrote a report warning that he was highly likely to be too arrogant. Next thing I knew, my client had hired him anyway. True love! For the next couple of months, I would hear about the horror stories from other managers and the human resources manager. He "knew everything better than anyone else" and when he made a mistake, he blamed it on poor information. He finally got the boot after a couple of months. Because he was a senior manager, he severely disrupted production for several months and frustrated many hard working people. Sure, managers need to be self-confident, but not to extremes.

You may wonder why that client ignored the test results and my advice–so do I. But over time, I find that clients start to believe what shows up in that personality crystal ball, and that is when things improve dramatically.

A company won't run on all cylinders if people are hired for jobs that don't quite fit and are uncomfortable with them. If the company was a TV screen, it would look blurred. A fuzzy alignment of personalities can greatly reduce profits, and when a few wolves and time are added to the mix, down she goes!

The Cost of Wrong Personality Hires

If you hire someone with extreme traits, you have almost the same problems as hiring a wolf. Thankfully, the problem is usually obvious and you will feel motivated to remove them in the first ninety days. These people waste others' time, cost money for training, disrupt the organization, and frustrate many. In larger companies, the problem is much more serious because the supervisors are not motivated to confront and fire them within those first ninety days.

When you hire people who don't fit the ideal personality profile for a job, you lose from their lack of drive, interest, and involvement. The cost for that is continuous, but not bad enough to fire. After several years of frustration on both sides, the employee may leave. So there are costs for retraining, but the biggest cost comes from a continuous inefficiency. If a high percentage of the workforce doesn't quite fit, the company can start losing money the moment there is an economic downturn.

On the other hand, you can learn about personality influences and take advantage of hiring those who love to do their jobs well.

The Main Personality Drives are Easy to Learn

You don't need to be a psychologist to understand personality profiles. There are four main profiles (Quadrants) you need to know about. It fits the "keep it simple stupid" formula. Study the rest of this chapter and pay attention to the people around you for practice, and you will have a working knowledge of profiles.

I have taught these four quadrants to many people and it doesn't take long to learn. Once you get the hang of them, you will be watching for them in applicants and everyone else. You will become the victor by hiring people into their strong areas. Not only will your success and profits increase, but your people will also prosper. This is truly a win-win deal.

The Personality Quadrants

Each quadrant is made up of about five personality traits. And each person is strongly driven by one of those quadrants (sometimes two). Rarely is a person strong in three quadrants or evenly spread over all quadrants. I will take you through each one and maybe you will recognize which one drives you. Keep asking yourself if the description speaks to you. The one that seems to be most like you will be your quadrant.

Let's start with the ANALYZER/LOGICAL quadrant. Dan the Computer Man operates a bit like the computers he loves to operate, fix and tweak. Quietly working in the back office going through the same old daily grind, he spends his time calibrating everything in sight. He also likes helping in the accounting department. He is a nice guy and says good morning if you can hear him. Talking with coworkers, he makes logical points and when they disagree, he can't understand how emotion has anything to do with anything. Dan is Mr. Predictable and keeps the computers and equipment running like Swiss watches.

Now for the CONTROLLER/ASSERTIVE quadrant, Harold Jones sits behind a huge desk pounding his fist while he tells one of his managers to improve production by ten percent —or else! Later in the day, Harold makes an on-the-spot decision to reduce costs by going with a cheaper employee medical plan. As the Human Resource manager tries to explain some of the disadvantages, he completely ignores her. He likes to get involved in closing the bigger sales deals. Harold has personal magnetism and makes the stockholders happy campers.

Ms. EXPRESSIVE/SOCIAL quadrant is next. Sandy Buttercup, the social butterfly, is late as usual, talking on her cell phone as another incoming call for her is announced over the intercom. Sandy is dressed to kill as she leaves for her sales calls. Talking to the customer at a mile a minute, she fails to hear anything the customer says. She fills in the order form – sort of.

Sandy is Ms popular, the life of the party, and sells more than the company can ever produce.

Last but not least, we have the SUPPORTER/EMPATHY quadrant. Suzie Que, the Social worker, is always volunteering to help. She doesn't know how to say "No." She spoils the kids at home and has a sympathetic ear for coworkers and clients alike. Although she is stretched thin helping, everyone loves her.

So in a nutshell, the CONTROLLER/ASSERTIVE runs the business and the EXPRESSIVE/SOCIAL keeps the orders coming in. The ANALYZER/LOGICAL makes the products and the SUPPORTER/EMPATHY is better suited to handle customer service. So how do you accurately identify a person's quadrant?

How to Interpret a Person's Quadrant

It takes a closer look to truly understand a person's quadrant. For example, people from all quadrants enjoy computers. However, the ANALYZER/LOGICAL is more likely drawn to fixing or calibrating them or working on excel spreadsheets. The EXPRESSIVE/SOCIAL likes sending e-mails from a computer while talking on the phone at the same time. The SUPPORTER/EMPATHY may use a computer to visit Greenpeace-type web sites. The CONTROLLER/ASSERTIVE will be looking up business and financial web sites. It's all a matter of observing what the person enjoys doing.

Understanding another's quadrant also depends on comparisons to others. For example, let's examine a person's desk. People from all quadrants can have a messy desk. The ANALYZER/LOGICAL is more likely to have a more organized desk than the EXPRESSIVE/SOCIAL. One way to tell a person's quadrant is to compare them to others.

Everyone operates in the other quadrants from time to time. But most of the time will act out their own quadrant. For example, an ANALYZER/LOGICAL will sometimes talk and talk but spend most of the time quietly doing technical work. Compared to the EXPRESSIVE/SOCIAL, this person says very little.

The Nitty Gritty Details

If one of the previous descriptions seems to fit you, find the quadrant following and examine the details. If you are an ANALYZER/LOGICAL, you will probably say, "Gee whiz just what I was hoping for, details!!" An EXPRESSIVE/SOCIAL will probably say, "Details–Ugh–I already have the gist of it, so I'll just gloss over this section. Or, on second thought, I will skip this section and use it when I need it." The other two quadrants could go either way.

Analyzer/Logical Quadrant

Basic tendencies (always present): A comfort and interest in being methodical. For example, likes getting paperwork organized for tax season. Those in other quadrants may do the same thing, but procrastinate to the last minute and hate messing with the details.

Tendencies (but not always): An interest in doing detail or technical work, usually in a serious, methodical, logical and exacting way. For example, will spend extra time making sure the checkbook is balanced to the penny, will feel a desire to be practical, persistent, and orderly, will also feel a strong desire to schedule tasks and do things right. If they go to a workshop, they like to take notes. These people are more focused than others on how things were done in the past.

Usual description: An introvert with a tendency to want to get administrative or manual work done well.

What the trait is not: This quadrant doesn't measure a person's ability or skill to organize, plan, see detail, or see mistakes. They have an interest and drive to do these things and are usually good at them. Even though a person in this quadrant has a comfort in being methodical or logical, it does not mean they are emotionless.

Closely related personality traits: Organization, Attention to Detail, Desire to get Paperwork done, Careful.

They are deficient in these traits: Desiring to Talk, Being Warm and Sociable, Meeting Strangers, Seeing the bigger picture, Taking risks.

Most suitable occupations for this quadrant: Accountant, bookkeeper, engineer, estimator, administrator, process coordinator, technical writer, programmer, systems analyzer, researcher, technical person, tradesperson.

Occupations to avoid: Salesperson, public speaker.

Other names for this quadrant: Analyzer, Gloomy, Beaver. (The names in this section are not mine. I included them because some people like them. Also, they help to describe the quadrant).

Logical vs Emotional: This is a logical and idea oriented quadrant.

Controller/Assertive Quadrant

Basic tendencies (always present): A comfort and interest in persuading others and getting things done ASAP. This is the leadership drive. For example, the person wants to keep things moving and will speak up about it.

Tendencies (but not always): A comfort and interest to be in charge of people and to get things done according to her plan. When a small group of people get together for the first time, she will try to elect herself president and feel desire to make decisions, make demands, and work toward achieving goals. This person feels more comfortable than others do when it comes to getting in the face of those who are slow, sloppy, or sneaky.

Usual description: Impatience with those who don't get things done yesterday and a desire to get in the face of those who fail to meet her expectations.

What the trait is not: This quadrant doesn't measure a person's ability or skill to sell, manage people, or get work done. However, the person is likely to be effective at these functions.

Closely related traits: assertiveness, competitiveness, impatience, sense of urgency, willingness to confront people, self-confidence, willingness to make decisions.

They are deficient in the following traits: empathy, patience, appreciation, willingness to listen, and tolerance of other's faults.

Most suitable occupations for this quadrant: Leader, team leader, sports coach, sales manager, salesperson, business leader, manager of supervisors, supervisor, project manager, court attorney, sales closer.

Occupations to avoid: Supporter (customer service) and a one-on-one coach.

Other names for this quadrant: Driver, Stormy, Lion.

Logical vs Emotional: This is a logical and idea oriented quadrant.

Expressive/Social Quadrant

Basic tendencies (always present): A comfort and interest in talking, telling, promoting and being sociable. They will get into conversations with strangers while waiting in line. People in other quadrants cannot understand this behavior.

Tendencies (but not always): A comfort and interest in talking and telling more than listening. This type of person is usually "fun loving," "extroverted," "group oriented," and likes "taking risks," "having fun," "enjoys change."

Usual descriptions: Spontaneous and often personally disorganized and comfortable mixing and interacting with complete strangers. They are known as Social Butterflies. They avoid detail work such as filling in forms and balancing checkbooks. Reading all these details is a pain for everyone, especially for them.

What the trait is not: This quadrant doesn't measure a person's ability or skill to communicate. However, most people in this quadrant are savvy about verbally getting ideas across well. (They go to communication workshops to learn how to listen–but only the most self-disciplined improve.)

Closely related traits: Desire to talk, Warm and Sociable, Willingness to Meet Strangers, Impulsive.

They are deficient in these traits: Willingness to Listen, Organization, Desire to do Attention to Detail, Getting Paperwork done, Methodical.

Most suitable occupations for this quadrant: Salesperson, lecturer, teacher to groups, politician, public relations, public announcer, advertiser, fiction writer, comedian and actor.

Occupations to avoid: Technical, engineer, accountant. (If you are an expressive person, learning the details about yourself can be challenging. I commend you for making it so far through all these details. Congratulations, you may be the only EXPRESSIVE/SOCIAL who did.)

Other names for this quadrant: Expressive, Sunny, Otters.

Logical vs Emotional: This is an emotion and feeling oriented quadrant.

Supporter/Empathy Quadrant

Basic tendencies (always present): An interest in pleasing and comforting other people. These are great people to be around when you are sick. They will feel sorry for you, offer to help you in any way they can, and when you ask them for a favor, nothing will be too much for them.

Tendencies (but not always): A comfort and interest in caring for other people and reluctance to direct others. A comfort and interest in listening, being patient, tolerant, and appreciative of other people. They have developed a great skill in putting off necessary confrontations. They have more excuses for not confronting someone than could fit on the internet.

Usual description: Loyal and adaptable. Wants to keep things the way they are.

What the trait is not: This quadrant doesn't measure a person's ability or skill to effectively help.

Closely related traits: empathy, patience, appreciation, willingness to listen, avoidance of confrontation and journey travelers (likes to smell the flowers on the way).

They are deficient in these traits: assertiveness, competitiveness, sense of urgency, willingness to confront people, self-confidence, and decision making.

Most suitable occupations for this quadrant: nurse, social worker, one-on-one coach, trainer, customer service person, sales clerk, technical support person, health care assistant, receptionist.

Occupations to avoid: courtroom attorney, sales closer, sales manager, manager of other supervisors, leader.

Other names for this quadrant: amiable, foggy (I would have thought calm was more accurate than foggy), Golden Retriever.

Logical vs Emotional: This is an emotional and feeling oriented quadrant.

The Details are Over

Welcome back all those who couldn't face the wall of details. Those who did—deserve a special award, especially the EXPRESSIVE/SOCIALS. Reading the definitions of each quadrant is like reading a dictionary. I don't think even the ANALYZER/LOGICALS would get far reading a dictionary. But, dictionaries are easier to read when you have a word you want to look up. To learn an uncommon word sometimes takes looking it up more than once. Treat the above explanations of the quadrants just as if you would use a dictionary. Look up the details when you need to hire someone.

Diagonal Opposites

Once you find someone's quadrant, the diagonal opposite will be her weakest. In other words, a person's weakest quadrant is usually diagonally opposite his strongest quadrant. For example, a person who is mainly an Analyzer type will feel very uncomfortable trying to be the Expressive type (diagonal opposite). In other words, an engineer makes a poor salesperson. If you hire these people as salespeople, they will do very poorly and won't last very long. The Controller and the Supporter are also opposites.

The personality types are diagrammed like this:

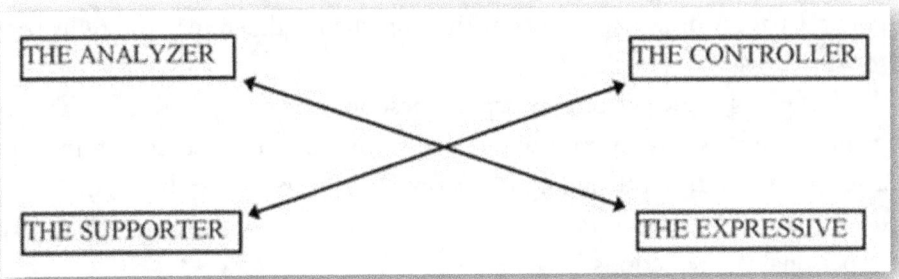

Understanding the diagonals helps predict future behavior. For example, if you know a person is strong in one quadrant you can expect weakness in the diagonal opposite.

On a personal note, it seems that most successful marriages are made up of people who are opposite in their main quadrant. This must be what they mean by the saying "opposites attract." When it comes to best friends, mine have always been in the opposite quadrant to me. But, I have been told by clients their best friends can be in any quadrant. One thing I know for sure is that relationships and friends seem to have similar core values.

The opposite-quadrant theory is important to the hiring process. Just as you need to know who to hire for certain jobs, you also need to know who not to hire. In working out who to hire, the most important thing to consider is what personality type the candidate must NOT be. For example, a strong Analyzer type makes a lousy salesperson, no matter how well he knows the product. He will most likely feel uncomfortable talking, making phone calls, promoting, and socializing. Verify a person's main quadrant by observing the diagonal opposite indicators.

A client of mine in a sales organization noted that whenever they hired a strong Analyzer type as a salesperson, it never worked out. He found that hiring people in the other three quadrants was successful. The best salespeople are mainly Expressive, Controller types (mixture of the two). Since the Analyzer personality is diagonally opposite the Expressive type, it follows that the best salespeople are weak in analyzing qualities. For example, they procrastinate when it comes to filling in forms or they fill them in poorly. If you're checking into a sales applicant and a reference mentions that he or she puts off paperwork, you have confirmation the candidate has the right personality drive.

Detecting these personality types is best done by using personality assessments. The best way to learn about the quadrants is to keep comparing the assessment results to the quadrant descriptions. Just by doing this, your hiring decisions will be a lot more accurate. As a bonus, you will become an expert in personality predictions.

To get a jump-start on learning the quadrants, do my written personality assessment on yourself. This will help you get a much better reality on the quadrants. You will start to understand why you do some of the things you do. Your personal understanding will help you understand these quadrants faster.

Connecting the Dots

As you can see in the description of each quadrant, there is a category called, "Most suitable occupations for this quadrant." One or more of the positions listed are those people feel motivated to do, even though they may not realize it. Therefore, before you start looking to fill a position, find the ideal quadrant or quadrants for it. (Sometimes one main quadrant will do sometimes two, but never three or four.)

Let's look at an example of how this idea could be applied to real life. You are looking for a salesperson for a job that requires strong closing requirements. You look under the EXPRESSIVE/SOCIAL quadrant and find 'salesperson' and under the CONTROLLER/ASSERTIVE you will find 'salesperson' and 'sales closer.' Yes, the perfect description. One thing you know for sure is that the opposite SUPPORTER/EMPATHY definitely won't work. You notice an EXPRESSIVE/SOCIAL could be a salesperson but the requirement calls for sales closing. So, you figure an ideal candidate may be strong on the right side quadrants and weak on the left side with more strength toward the CONTROLLER/ASSERTIVE. You may run into a problem finding someone who has the drive of a sales manager to take a salesperson position.

Sometimes it pays to rearrange the job so that someone sells the customer and the manager helps on the close.

Okay, you're sold on the value of quadrants, now to discover the best ways to figure out a person's quadrant.

How to Figure out a Person's Quadrant

Past behavior is supposed to be the best predictor of future behavior. And because a quadrant drives behavior, a past drive is the best predictor of a future drive. Therefore, you need to find out what sort of major activities the person enjoyed (enjoyed is the key here) doing. Also, find out which activities they didn't enjoy as much. By comparing the activities the person enjoyed doing with the quadrant descriptions, you should be able to get a sense of what drives the person. To confirm what you found, the activities that bored the person should be the diagonal opposites.

Another way of finding out a person's quadrant is to ask what activities he is interested in doing. For example, ask the applicant, "What do you like doing most on a computer?" or, "How do you like using spreadsheets compared to visiting web sites?" or, "What type of web sites do you normally visit?" Compare his answers to the quadrant descriptions.

Other good subjects to ask applicants about: (Good confirmation questions when you take the candidate for lunch before you make them an offer.)

* Going to parties or staying home doing what?
* Talking to strangers waiting in line or doing what?
* Influencing the direction of a small group of people you are involved in or doing what?
* Helping others by being sympathetic or using tough love or what?
* Taking detail notes when attending a workshop or what?

By asking people these questions, you will get a sense of which quadrant they operate from. A more direct and time saving way, especially when you start down this road, is to give them personality assessments that also measure quadrants.

The Crystal Ball

When giving fish to the poor, would you prefer to just give them the fish or would you rather teach them to fish for themselves? I prefer teaching them, but I have to keep them alive until they learn. The best way I can teach you about personalities is to encourage you to use my personality assessments when hiring. Why? Because you will immediately start to see the benefits of knowing what drives people. You will also learn to use and get the benefits of everything covered in this chapter.

The greatest benefits from getting candidates to do the assessments are as follows:

* Accuracy in determining a person's personality drives.
* Detection of any extreme personality traits that otherwise would have remained hidden.
* Insurance against hiring someone who wouldn't fit the job.
* Time saved in interviewing.
* Way to learn more about personalities and how to read them.

I designed personality assessments for business use rather than a psychological tool. The results come out in plain English that are easily understood. A manual and a free help line are available to explain the results if there are any questions. You will find out about twenty different personality traits, and it will uncover any extreme traits. You will learn the person's main quadrant and back up quadrants. The questionnaires can be taken online, or on paper and faxed, or by e-mail attachments. They are priced for volume use, so employers can easily afford to use them on all those that look good after the first interview.

Wolves and Personalities

The personality profile of a person is completely different from his or her attitude. A wolf can come in any one of the quadrants. Even the SUPPORTER/ EMPATHY can be a wolf by feeling sorry for other wolves and supporting them. If it wasn't for attitudes, even the inexperienced could detect a quadrant without much trouble. But when you add attitudes into the mix, it does become more complicated. For example, a CONTROLLER/ASSERTIVE may become impatient with someone, which could be interpreted as a mean, nasty person, when in reality it is just a personality characteristic.

Knowledge of personality types is NOT limited to hiring. You can also use it for promoting or changing existing employees.

Promote by Personality

When you need to change or promote an employee, you may be wise to do so after knowing her two strongest quadrants. Just because a person does well as an individual contributor does not mean she will do well as a supervisor. I know you know this, but I also know this mistake is made over and over again. A wiser move is to have the person do the personality assessments and see if she has what it takes to manage people.

Even if you are forced to promote someone, you will at least know what to keep an eye on. For example, you promote a person to supervisor, but the assessment indicates a great reluctance to confront someone—the "nice guy finishes last" syndrome. Now you know that whenever disciplinary matters come up, someone else will need to be the heavy.

Sometimes you need to increase a person's responsibility, but the answer is not always a promotion. Spend more time being creative about such decisions. Instead of making the person a supervisor, make them a lead. Alternatively, change her job to one that may fit her personality. Use the power of personalities as a win-win move for both employer and employee.

My Cup Runneth Over

My clients who understand and apply the last three chapters experience the benefits of correct size pegs in correct size holes. They also have good-natured, hard-working people who are loyal and support them. What a relief! These employees aren't perfect, but their average quality is so much higher than their competitors, it gives an employer a definite advantage. If business people weren't so superstitious, you would see them dancing around saying, "My Cup Runneth Over."

Where Do We Go From Here?

The remainder of this book describes the specific steps to hiring good people. The following nine chapters are written in the sequence necessary to hire someone. When you need to hire someone, you can study chapter four and do what it says. When you've done that, you can study Chapter Five and apply that and so on. Keep doing this with the next applicant. This may seem too slow and it is. But it will take some effort to improve the process.

A long time ago, I learned a valuable rule: THE NUMBER OF TIMES YOU STUDY THE SAME THING, THE BETTER RESULTS YOU WILL GET FROM IT. It sounds boring, I know, but the ring of the cash register makes up for a lot. This concept applies to the subject of this book. Keep reading it and applying the ideas until you hire truly great people on a consistent basis.

Chapter 4

What Does the Ideal Candidate for the Job Look Like?

Finding a talent team player starts by describing the ideal person for the job. Because we don't live in a world of perfect people, this is the most creative step in the hiring process. You will need to consider top priority traits and traits that don't really matter. You may need to throw out ideas that have worked in the past. You may have to think of different ways to skin the elephant. Whatever you come up with, the end result of your creative thinking should be a written description.

This description, written out, is called the profile. It is the description of the skills, experience, education, attitude and personality required for a given job. It can include familiarity with machines and software, performance goals, pay range, literacy level, licenses, and even the applicant's philosophical points of view or anything else you feel is important. It also includes traits that would be nice, but not required, traits that don't matter, and bad traits to be avoided. See samples of profiles at the back of this chapter.

Why Work Out a Profile?

Why do people draw up plans before they build a house? Why don't they just build the house and design it as they go along? Think of all the money and time saved in designing? Many of us would like to believe design is unnecessary but as we get older, we realize how valuable the planning stage is. Hiring people is no different; you will do better with a plan, especially if you are going after super people.

I see business people make this failure-to-plan mistake too many times. They start out looking for superwoman or superman and after weeks, sometimes months, realize she or he is not out there. This would be like getting the walls up without a plan and realizing there is no room for a bathroom. Because I am in the testing business, I sometimes get a "Help" type phone call. "Your tests" they blame, "I have eliminated all my candidates!" Well, it usually turns out they want the rare or impossible, such as a strong administrative person who can sell meat to vegetarians.

Super people are only great for the job they fit and will do well. I was in a restaurant recently and saw a good example of this in their buss boy. He was obviously a little mentally slow but had a great manner about him and did a good job. My guess is he will stay for a long time, happy to have a job, and the restaurant will not have to worry about that function. Go into one of America's most successful businesses, Wal-Mart, and talk to some of their employees. I found some had trouble speaking English but for a little above minimum wage, they seem very productive. Designing the requirements is not about wanting the best of everything and expecting to pay for the minimum.

The best way to design what you need is to develop a realistic profile. I can understand how busy you are, so why would you want to go to the trouble of doing more paperwork? The same reason someone would draw up plans to build a house. You don't want to get into advertising, resume reading, and interviewing only to realize the direction you are going won't work.

Developing a profile helps you consider the type of people available in the work force and how much you are willing to pay. You may even have to redesign the job to get what you want. But once you have your plan, you are ready to go. You will have a better chance of starting your search in the right direction. You will have a better chance that the candidate will do well over the long haul. And you won't need to look back later and say to yourself, "What was I thinking!"

Other Reasons to Consider Doing a Profile

First off, we all have an idea of whom we're looking for in a job applicant, but that's the point. We only have an idea. Since it's usually a rough idea and since the description of the super candidate is specific, it is easier to chase after people who won't fit. Take personality, for example; if you don't have that clearly worked out, you may end up hiring someone who doesn't like his job. We know what that means. The candidate that fits the profile, on the other hand, will do a good job, will feel at home doing the job and will stay motivated and productive for a long time.

Secondly, a profile also helps you stay focused in the hiring process. It helps you design the right ads, what to look for in resumes, what to ask recruiters or personnel people and what to ask in interviews. I've seen companies actively advertising, testing, interviewing and reference checking only to hire the wrong person. The profile had never been closely examined.

Thirdly, because you researched and thought about those you want, you will reduce the chance of eliminating candidates for faults that don't matter. Because finding good people is usually your biggest challenge, this will open up valuable opportunities.

Fourthly, because you may miss some important aspects, you can use the profile as a check off sheet. In this way, you are more likely to remember important questions to ask and areas to examine.

Fifthly, one of the common interviewing faults is falling in love with a candidate too early on in the interview process. In addition, if the manager really needs someone, she will want to believe she has the right person. These two reasons will cause most managers to overlook any faults. However, with a profile, you're more likely to be aware of all the traits you'll need and less likely to overlook them. On the other hand, working out a profile after you think you've found the perfect candidate is a waste of time because it is human nature to design the profile to match the candidate.

Sixthly, once you have a profile worked out for a position, especially one that has a lot of turnover, you will not have to do it again. Or if the people fit the profile but fail, then you know the profile or the position needs to be changed.

The Four Basic Personalities

The four quadrants, explained in the previous chapter, play a big role in working out a profile. I suggest you refer back to that chapter when working out the profile with special reference to the type of jobs and activities that match the profile. In working out a profile, the most important thing to consider is what personality type the candidate must *not* be. For example, strong Analyzer types will make lousy salespeople, no matter how well they know the product. They'll likely experience difficulty with building relationships quickly, talking, promoting, and socializing.

The "Perfect" Candidate

The first thing to know is that there are no "perfect candidates." If interviewers think they have found these "perfect candidates" after interviewing, and I know how easy that is, they are more than likely being too superficial, and the candidates are doing a great sales job. These so-called "perfect candidates" always end up having flaws after they're hired, though some, with luck, turn out to be good employees.

In designing a profile or looking for someone to fill a position, you should be willing to acknowledge which areas the best personality for the position are likely to be lacking. For example, when looking for a salesperson, their main personality style shouldn't be that of an Analyzer. Therefore, you should appreciate the fact that a sales candidate puts off doing his paperwork. That indicator is a sign he is an Expressive/Social who feels comfortable calling customers on the phone, promoting for business, and talking. A bad trait for one job can be a good trait for another.

Don't try to find people who can do and be everything because they would probably be overqualified.

Culture

Culture is the set of values that management believes are important for the company's success. When interviewing, be especially alert for applicants who wouldn't be compatible with the company values. If the company is new and the culture is one of trying new things, taking risks, and working long hours, then the candidate should fit into this mind set.

Other examples of a culture include:

* An old, established company may have a culture of taking few risks, not rocking the boat, not working too hard, following procedures exactly, and not doing anything new and unusual. A new employee, for example, who wants to come in with big plans to modernize the business—when the business owner just wants to retire in a few years without any changes—won't work.
* Company management may believe the customer is always right and do everything necessary to treat the customer as king. An applicant who feels customers can't be trusted and that they need to be corrected "because they are seldom right" would be a terrible selection.
* Management may believe supervisors should take more responsibility and make decisions rather than need detailed instructions. A poor supervisor for this company would be someone afraid to take risks or make decisions without checking with the boss first.
* Ethical and moral standards vary from company to company and person to person. An applicant who believes it is Okay to be late on customer deliveries will do poorly in a company that prides itself on delivering on time.

Be aware of the culture of your company and your department. This culture should be part of the profile with minor changes from department to department. Fortunately, once the culture has been identified, it is easy to attach to future profiles. See the section on culture in Chapter Eleven, "Interviewing Questions."

How to Develop a Profile

A profile is developed from examining those employees who've been successful and then making a note of their common traits. Examining the worst employees is also very useful for pinpointing traits the applicant must not have.

You can also get this information by examining employees in other businesses in the same line of work. With some minor adjustments, the sample profiles at the end of this chapter can be models for your profiles.

The next step is to list all the job functions that go with the position; the job description should help in doing this. The job functions are not part of the profile, but the skills and knowledge an applicant should have to do them is. In cases where you're hoping to promote the person to a final position in a series of jobs, you should also consider the profile for the last position. List the skills and knowledge that you're prepared to teach under what would be nice. The potential to learn these should be under what the person must have.

For example, you want to hire someone for your customer service desk to assist customers with technical questions, and you have a new and unique product. Because the person must be familiar with your product, and because your product is unique, you must hire someone and apprentice her on your product first before putting her on the customer service desk. Your profile would be for a customer service personality with the addition of *potential to learn your product* under the *Must Have* column. You should also list any abilities or potential abilities necessary to complete the apprentice program.

Some of the most important elements in a profile are the personality traits. One should start out with good and bad personality traits for a job, as described in the previous chapter. If you have jobs that don't fit any of the descriptions in the previous chapter, you will need to pick the closest ones.

When hiring people from outside your organization, it is important that they have track records of success in the positions being offered. The positions where this is most applicable are in sales, supervision and leadership. If a person has never sold before, then they have not established a track record. Therefore, hiring them as a salesperson would be a risk, even if they had the right personality. Some people can sell and others can't. If you are promoting a guy to sales within your organization, there is far less risk because you know his track record. Supervisors or managers can either supervise people or they can't. Leaders or general managers for remote offices can either lead or they can't. So your profile should have the appropriate track records under the *must have* column.

Don't include certain educational levels unless they're really important; your organization is an educational one or the applicant is young. Many people with high educational levels can't produce effective results. Instead,[1] you may want to describe what you expect a person with a given education should be able to do or understand and include that in your requirements.

Don't assume something is a requirement until you've carefully checked it out as described above.

Jobs that Need a Profile

Jobs that make up a major percentage of your workforce need profiles. For example, in a sales organization, a profile of a successful salesperson would be essential. Jobs that have had a high turnover should have profiles, as should supervisory, managerial and executive positions. It's also a good idea to work out the profiles for the remaining positions as time and resources are available. In time, you'll have a good inventory of profiles to use.

Designing the profile should be viewed as your tactical planning for a profitable business or department.

The following list may help jog your mind for what may be needed on a profile.

Checklist of Possible Items for Profiles

- Intelligence
- Right personality profile for the position
- All applicable skills
- Licenses and diplomas for the position
- Creativity
- Can strategically plan
- Pragmatic
- Oral communications
- Written communications

* Education
* Relevant job experience
* Software experience
* Quality standards meeting company's standards
* Customer service matching company standard
* Organized
* Dependable
* Self-motivated
* Successful track record
* Good overall presentation
* Enthusiasm
* Likable
* Empathy
* Assertiveness
* Negotiation skills
* Savvy to customer needs
* Political business savvy
* Ambitious
* Realistic risk taker
* Good health (certain jobs)
* Patient
* Competitive
* Confident
* Likes working inside
* Like working outside
* Ability to focus on the job
* Warm and friendly
* Conceptual ability
* Not a 'yes' person
* Pay range
* Ability to focus on important priorities without being distracted by busy work, etc.
* Keeps up-to-date with profession
* Hard worker

* Has initiative to seek out opportunities
* Doesn't lose temper easily
* Likes doing paperwork
* Correct personality for the position
* Willing to admit personal faults without rationalizing
* Willing to make adjustments
* Honest and trustworthy
* Cooperative and supportive of bosses
* Realistic expectations of the company and employees
* Drug-free
* Appreciative
* Problem solver
* Social perceptiveness
* Stable
* Persistent
* Mature
* Machine skills

Profile Set Up

The profile is best set up into four columns. The first column would cover those traits, skills, and experiences that are essential for the position. The title of that column is "Must Have." The second column of traits describing what would be preferable, but not mandatory, is called "Nice to Have." The third column is "Doesn't Matter." The fourth column would cover traits the candidate must not have. The title of that column is "Absolutely Not." Before reading further, turn to the sample profiles at the end of the chapter to familiarize yourself with how to set them up.

Why the Profile Should be Very Detailed

One serious bad trait is all it takes to make an employee a bad hire. If the candidate doesn't have all the traits listed, you run the risk of completely overlooking a bad trait or several. For example, if the profile requires the employee to be able to write but he can't, this person wouldn't work out. If that trait isn't listed on the profile, a bad hire could result.

The *Doesn't Matter* column is needed for traits that could be considered important but actually aren't. Having a *Doesn't Matter* column can prevent an otherwise good candidate from being turned down.

If you think of a trait that should be under the *Must Have* column, but you can't think how to verify that trait, put it down anyway. How to interview for or verify a trait is a different activity. Coming up with creative ways to verify traits should be done after you acknowledge what is needed on a profile.

Consult a Hiring Expert

If you're trying to work out a profile you're not completely familiar with, consult someone who is familiar. This input will be invaluable to you. A manager trying to hire a salesperson for the first few times, for example, can easily think of traits that are unnecessary for the job. With advice, research and experience, the true profile will continue to become clearer.

Resume Requirements

The profile should contain several items that would show up on resumes, such as *two years minimum experience as a full charge bookkeeper*. You can easily check this item on a resume, which helps narrow down those who are qualified.

Be careful not to overdo it in this area that you disqualify the majority of your candidates. Only put down the absolute necessary work experiences.

Balance of Personality Types

Sometimes a department needs a certain type of personality to balance another. A client of mine, an Expressive with some Controller, made one of his best decisions by hiring a manager with the opposite Analyzer/Logical personality. My client was creative, and the Analyzer was organized and detail-oriented. They complemented each other and did extremely well as a team. To make the best use of your profiles, remember to keep in mind the most effective balance for the whole department or organization.

Legal

A non-discriminatory profile will help protect you from possible legal attacks. It's another way to help keep your employees doing the legal thing. Also, don't exclude people with disabilities in your profile. See Chapter Thirteen, "Legal Issues," for further information.

Assessments, Tests and the Profile

The profile is even more valuable to those employers who use tests or assessment. After you have completed the profile, you need to decide which traits, skills, and knowledge need to be tested. Select the tests or assessments to cover the appropriate areas and give them to all those applicants with a good possibility of being the right one. If you use assessments, you should always include ones that measure personality types.

Profiles as the New Wave

The profile is coming into use more as personality assessments become more popular. After working with a profile for a while, you'll make adjustments and your selection process will continue to improve.

Use the sample profiles that follow to work out your positions. Just copy the applicable page and then make adjustments by crossing out what doesn't fit and adding what is needed in the space provided.

Profiles to Adjust to Your Requirements

Salesperson

Sample Profile #1

This sample profile would best suit *sales people* who sell and close sales—not just take orders and do retail sales (which usually demand little more than taking orders).

Must Haves	Nice to Have	Doesn't matter	Absolutely Not
assertive	good listener	advance educational degrees	meek
good communicator	hard worker	detail oriented	9-to-5 mentality
mentally quick	completed high school	patient	bad attitude
impulsive	industry experience	has paperwork avoidance	shy
persuasive	competitive	high intelligence	has analyzer logical personality
willing to travel	warm and friendly	organized	overly exaggerates everything
willing to work base plus commission	animated		drug user
literate to eighth grade level	expressive social personality		is not worse than an average liar
self-starter	builds rapport quickly		
minimum of two years of successful sales track record			
interested in the job			
measurable results produced			
willing to do necessary paperwork			
prefers to work for commission			

If you feel some of the items in the *Doesn't Matter* column should be in the *Must Have* column, you could be looking for perfect candidates rather than profitable ones. For example, in sales, a poor listener does have the advantage of ignoring the effects of negativity. Being a good listener belongs in the *Nice to Have* column as it can be helpful, though few practicing salespeople are good listeners. Successful ones test strongly on talking and weakly on listening.

Intelligence is another item one might expect to be in the *Must Have* column, there is little or no difference in good or poor salespeople based on their intelligence. In testing sample groups, I saw little difference between good salespeople with high or low IQs.

Manager or Supervisor

Sample Profile #2

This sample profile would best suit *managers or supervisors* with more than three people reporting to them, such as, a store manager for a service unit with twenty to thirty-five employees and a high customer service corporate culture. Project leaders or individual contributors with one or two assistants should have a different profile.

Must Haves	Nice to Have	Doesn't Matter	Absolutely Not
has supervised 16 people at one time	good math skills	shy but not timid	unassertive
high school level writing skills	hard worker	high level of education	unwilling to wear a tie
assertive	experience in your industry	patient	mainly supporter empathy personality
proven success as a manager	organized		needs constant direction and supervision
ambitious	attention to detail		has a bad attitude
has reasonable desire to complete paperwork	promotes a sense of urgency		argumentative
knows how to delegate	empathy for others		dishonest
believes customer service is extremely important	will find and hold out to hire great people		uses drugs
intelligent	good trainer and coach		
compensation plan fits life style and desires	effective at setting appropriate expectations		
good planner	looks presentable		
willing to confront negativity	builds excellent rapport with direct reports		
considers management an ideal job	encourages employee participation		
pragmatic	is good at keeping team informed of company objectives and activities		

Manufacturing Manager

Sample Profile #3

This sample profile would best suit *managers* with supervisors reporting to them, such as, a manufacturing manager of a machine shop with ten to twenty employees, with a corporate culture of working long hours and some weekends. This profile would not work well for project leaders or individual contributors with one or two assistants.

Must Haves	Nice To Have	Doesn't Matter	Absolutely Not
2 years minimum experience dealing with people (sales, CSR, admin, etc)	knowledge of companies' software systems	advanced education	augmentative
comfortable on the phone	computer science background	paperwork avoidance	downplays other team players and builds self up
patient	pays attention to details	well organized	combative
one year or more experience with HTML or related software coding	successful experience in customer services		aggressive
speaks clearly	intelligent		controller / assertive personality
dependable	empathy for others		programmer type personality
responsive			user of drugs
good attitude			negative about company
good listener			
warm with people			
comfortable on the phone			
capable of staying focus on problems for long periods of time			
considers this an ideal job			
one year or more experience with HTML or related software coding			
bright and alert			

Bookkeeper

Sample Profile #4

This sample profile would work well for lesser *accounting functions* or for a controller (accounting title) or similar positions, such as a full charge bookkeeper for a small, twenty-employee company that is expanding at ten percent per year. This profile would not work well for other department heads.

Must Haves	Nice To Have	Doesn't Matter	Absolutely Not
likes detail work	one year experience with company's accounting software	good communication skills	expressive personality type
high intelligence	one year industry-specific experience	assertive	careless
likes rechecking work	likes improving processes	warm and friendly	needs constant supervision
honest	acceptable 10-key skill level	advance educational degrees	afraid of making routine collection calls
understands basic bookkeeping principles	organized		user of drugs
three years using QuickBooks or company specific software	highly literate		
good attitude			
believes bookkeeping is the ideal job			
can do sales taxes and quarterly reporting			
is the analyzer personality type			
has advanced excel skills			
good at math			
works well with others			

Technical Support

Sample Profile #5

This profile would work for *technical support positions,* like a customer service representative for a computer software company, and for *catalog salespeople* receiving in bound calls.

Must Haves	Nice To Have	Doesn't Matter	Absolutely Not
two-year minimum experience dealing with people (sales, reception, etc.)	knowledge of the company's software programs	education	argumentative
empathy for others	computer science background	paperwork avoidance	downplays other team players and builds self up
patient	pays attention to detail	sales ability	combative
bright and alert	successful experience in customer service	well-organized	aggressive
speaks clearly	intelligent	physical traits	controller / assertive personality as the main personality
dependable	empathy for others	race, age, gender, ethnic upbringing	programmer-type personality
responsive			user of illegal drugs
good attitude			puts the company down to others
good listener			
warm with people			
comfortable on the phone			
able to stay with a problem a long time			
considers this an ideal job			
one-plus years' experience in the company's computer language			

Chapter 5

Finding Profitable Candidates

Finding great people to interview is a major challenge. You can invest a lot of money doing it, and you need to be creative and be able to pull it off successfully. Using all the techniques currently in use, you will reduce your hiring costs and find better ways to beat the challenge.

The amount of money spent on finding candidates to interview is part of a company's culture. Some employers are only willing to place one small ad on a major job board like Careerbuilder.com. On the other hand, others are willing to pay thirty percent recruiter fees and the candidate's travel expenses. Some are willing to invest a lot while others as little as possible.

The new employer tends to economize on time and effort to get candidates. He runs an ad for a short time and gets "a good response." He usually believes the resume is mostly accurate. He also doesn't know how to get below the surface of a candidate's answers. He often ends up thinking he has more than one great applicant to decide from. In reality, he rarely finds even a mediocre person.

Confronting the result of interviewing takes up to a year and by that time, most managers are not connecting the feeble ad campaign to the result. It all gets shrugged off. The experienced managers have had it happen so many times they know better.

The successful small or large business owner is willing to pay good time and money for promising candidates. She knows the reality of hiring and is willing to spend what it takes to find good people. She also knows good employees make money and bad ones cost money.

Finding good applicants is usually only a matter of developing a simple marketing program and running it for a long enough period of time. It also requires a willingness to invest time and money up front, rather than heaps of money on poor hires.

Marketing Plan

Start by deciding what sort of marketing program you'll need. It may be as simple as putting out the word to your employees, or it could be as involved as designing ads and placing them in several places, using online ads, putting up signs or getting out the word to your suppliers, customers, and acquaintances. My clients found the following suggestions were the most helpful in the order that reflects the most successful results.

Referrals

The best employees come from referrals. Many times, I've asked a client where they got such a good employee, and most of the time they'll say from a referral, usually by another employee.

Great employees are usually happy with their company and are loyal, but some are not. They might dislike the existing management culture, need a change, or feel their current position isn't ideal. These great employees may not actively look for a change, but want to be approached about job opportunities. One bit of research, stated that 26% of the workforce look for another job at any point in time, but the best people are usually not part of that 26%. Therefore, approaching candidates, rather than advertising for them, increases your chances of hiring the best.

The best way to approach candidates is through networking. By networking I mean communicating with others for leads on candidates. For example, approach your own employees in the same type of position you are looking to fill and ask them if they know of anyone who would be good. When you have names, coach the employee to make contact and develop enough interest for a call.

Make announcements to your entire staff that you are looking for someone to fill a particular position and give them some basic requirements. Ask them, one-on-one, for people they may know. Keep reminding them that you're still looking for someone and let them know when you find a suitable candidate. You may want to keep the word out at all times if you're always looking for good people.

You can also ask people outside your company for referrals. In some businesses, vendor representatives know of people in competitor companies who aren't happy. Ask these vendors for referrals.

When you ask people for a referral, help stimulate their thinking. Help remind them of people they have known in the past who might be interested. Get them to think about people they talk to on a regular basis as a possibility.

The Human Resource Manager or the person in charge of hiring employees for the whole company should be effective at networking. For some hiring managers, it may take moving out of comfort zones to do this. When you get used to doing it, and learn how to do it well, it will become much easier.

I have seen plenty of candidates come highly recommended—superficially interviewed because "everyone knew they were good"—who had to be let go. But overall, the quality of referrals is higher than those responding to ads.

Therefore, if your company is suffering from a lack of good employees then check the networking activity. Or in the event that you are spending a lot of money on recruiters, you may also be wise to check into the company's networking efficiency.

Recruiters

If you can't find someone through referrals, your next best choice is through recruiters. They specialize in networking.

Recruiters may charge twenty to thirty percent of a candidate's first-year salary and benefits, which you pay after you accept and hire the candidate. The best recruiters will usually ask for non-refundable retainers. If they deliver quality applicants, it's a good investment. I've seen some very good candidates come from recruiters, but I've also seen many duds. Compared to job board advertising, the recruiter's candidates are much better, which means you don't need to deal with as many applicants.

I don't recommend recruiters if you and your managers are not experienced or trained at interviewing, experienced means having interviewed candidates for over a year. It also means that you and your managers are used to closely examining the outcomes of the interviews. Training is more than a one-day magic workshop. A realistic approach, not false confidence, is absolutely required. Paying thirty percent for a bad hire is a bad investment.

You probably already know this, but just in case, recruiters train their candidates to look their best in interviews. They'll also sell and persuade you to accept their candidates because they want their commission. Even the most ethical ones can't help exaggerating and covering up to get that pile of money. It's human nature.

Even a three-month guarantee may sound good, but real trouble can start after that period of time—especially attitude. It is easy for an experienced wolf to wait until the 90-day probationary period is over before relaxing back into his natural state. Also, most managers would rather not confront employees who exhibit negative behaviors, so they can get by the 90-day period. Don't rely on that guarantee.

If you have a good screening program, you can make good use of recruiters. Let them send those who have the skills and already have jobs. You screen out the incompetents, the poor attitude types and those not really interested in the position. Make the recruiters earn their commissions.

Recruiters are great at finding competent qualified candidates but horrible at discovering or disclosing attitude issues. Usually, they go after those who are already employed, which is more likely to produce good attitude candidates.

Recruiters can be efficiently used to find engineers, computer programmers, executives, salespeople, and other specialized workers.

Don't let recruiters do your reference checking for you. They usually get paid when someone is placed, so they can't be objective about a reference check. When recruiters have already done the reference check, it won't be as easy for you to then ask the same people for the same reference.

There are good recruiters and poor recruiters, just like in any other industry. Don't give up on using them over some bad experiences caused by one bad apple. Do background checks on the recruiters, as some will keep taking one person from company to company. Use them if you know how to spot attitude problems and interview well.

Job Fairs

There are companies that put on job fairs. They advertise these fairs to people looking at making a change in their careers. The companies interested in participating pay a fee to have a table at the fair. The people looking for a better job come with their resumes and meet the company representatives at their tables.

The advantage to employers is the ability to talk to potential applicants, to determine attitudes and competencies before time-consuming interviews take place. My clients in technology businesses tell me it is more successful than using recruiters.

Colleges and Universities

If your company can use recent college graduates, then contacting the appropriate colleges are a great plan and a good source of raw talent. Many college students don't know their potential. They also don't know who to work for when they graduate. Contacting them before they graduate could net you some super, long-term employees.

Target a college that specializes in your company's industry. As you know, colleges specialize in all sorts of industries, and you probably know the local ones in your field.

Trying this method requires some involvement beyond just posting a notice. It takes finding out what the school's program is for hiring. Some schools have special weeks of the year set up specifically for this purpose.

Getting to know the college professors who may be able to refer you to their best students is also effective.

If this method is unfamiliar to you, then find out more from the college and see what your competition or other companies are doing. Find out the professors' e-mail addresses or phone numbers and ask them if they know of anyone. Start the students out part-time while they are still going to college. In addition, before they graduate, offer them full-time positions.

Temporary Agencies

Another effective way to hire hourly people is through a temporary agency. You need to give those they send you a regular interview because these people can hide their bad traits like anyone else. Hire anyone who looks good and watch for performance and attitude. If they do poorly, have bad attitudes or lack interest, just send them back for another. Those that do well after a reasonable amount of time, you keep. The only catch is that you will need to pay the temporary agency's fee before you can take the person on as a regular employee.

By using the temporary agency method, you can keep positions covered faster and reduce hiring time and expense. When you send someone back, you're less exposed to legal problems because you're not firing anyone.

Employment agencies are good for administrative assistants, receptionists, and accounting, customer service and other hourly people.

Advertising for Applicants

Advertising for competent, good attitude people is less expensive than recruiters and temporary agencies, but it takes a lot more time. I've seen some excellent people hired from an ad; unfortunately, I've seen many more bad hires.

Advertising is good for new business owners or those on a budget who want experience in the hiring game. It will be more time consuming, less expensive and a good way to learn that all that glitters is not gold. Those you do hire can become your referral base. One good quality of poor hires is that their references sometimes turn out to be great employees.

Advertising a position seems to attract all those who don't get referred or who don't meet the minimum qualifications a recruiter would accept. When you run an ad, you may get dozens or even hundreds of resumes and phone calls. Many of the resumes won't be related to the position advertised, and those that do relate are likely to have attitude problems. Because of this, you must have an effective screening system if you want to advertise.

The key to advertising a job opening is casting the widest net possible. Following this strategy will hopefully produce a large number of applicants over a 30 day period and even more over 60 to 90 days. This creates a dilemma, a lot of work, with not enough time to sort through all these applicants it is critical to a have a strategy to screen resumes and talk to as many of the possibly qualified people. Make sure to read the next chapter on resume screening.

Because of the high volume of responses ads produce, you may be overwhelmed and choose a candidate out of self-preservation. So much attention goes into sorting the good from the bad, it becomes challenging to focus. As pressures increases from the empty position and the distraction of sorting out candidates, it takes a strong person to stay focused.

If you don't consider yourself a savvy hiring game player, join the crowd. This is a good way for you to hone your hiring skills, especially if you keep referring to hiring books.

Designing Ads

One good place to start is looking at ads placed for similar positions. You can Google the title of your position or go to any of the major job boards for examples. This will give you point of reference how others are doing it, not necessarily an example of the best way to create an ad.

Your ad should be in alignment with the profile covered in Chapter Four. The ad should also appeal to a person with a good attitude. Stressing money and big benefits is more likely to attract bad attitude applicants. Remember wolves have a much greater interest in what is in it for them.

The wording of the ad can make a big difference in the responses you get. Responses may range from about ten per week to about fifty per week just by changing the wording of the ad. Be willing to experiment until you get a good response.

The title of the position and the first word are very important. The first word is important because it places the ad in the area of the job board where competently qualified candidates are looking. The job title can change the response and applicability of candidates significantly. When I ran an ad with "Sales Consultant," I got applicants with strong sales backgrounds, just the type of people I wanted. When I ran an ad starting with "Management Consultant," I received more responses, but less people who fit the sales profile I was hoping for, even though the remainder of the ad was the same.

A fundamental principle in all advertising is attracting attention. Notice how advertisers get your attention on TV with beautiful bodies or unusual scenes. The message to their ads is different from what gets your attention in the first place. They need your attention first so that you will even notice their message. Now, notice how advertisers get attention in their employment ads. Do something to get your ad noticed you can do things like change the title fonts or upload your company's logo to accompany your ad.

Your ad must have good appeal to elicit a favorable response. Find out what seems most appealing about the position you're offering and mention that as close to the beginning of the ad as possible. For example, when I added "consultant possibilities" near the beginning of my ad, I got a much greater response. This is because most of the people I was advertising for liked the idea of being a consultant. Good candidates will be more interested in an exciting challenge than the money.

With that said, mention, but don't stress, what is in it for them. For example, you can mention secure position, friendly people, ethical environment, medical benefits, travel, car, and so forth. Don't leave things out that you feel are obvious because the readers are likely to think it is not part of the package.

You should cover somewhere in your ad three or four important experiences, skills or qualifications that the applicant must have. Look at the profile you developed for this position, but don't be too specific in your ad. For example, saying the applicant must know WordPerfect could eliminate great people who know other word processing programs very similar to WordPerfect. It would be better to say "minimum of one year experience in word processing." You want to open up the possibilities of finding qualified and good-natured people.

When describing job skills change them to describe performance requirements. For a sales person a job requirement might be' "Must have the ability develop relationships with key clients." Change this to say, "Develop relationships with key customers and increase revenue from those clients by 10% annually." For an accountant you may have a requirement of, "Must have the ability to complete and manage sale and use tax filings." Change this to say, "Complete sales and use tax filings within 15 days of filing deadlines." The more specific the expectations the easier it will be to determine if the candidate has the experience or skills to complete the tasks required.

Avoid any mention of attitude traits in your ads. Experience has taught me that most people don't know how they rate on attitude, and almost all people believe they have a much better attitude than they actually do. That is why ads must focus on skills. You can eliminate all those who don't have the skills, so you can focus on personality to select the best.

If you do work out an ad that produces, don't change it; try to improve it or vary the media. One changed word can make all the difference.

Check for Legality before Placing an Ad

Read through your ad looking for legal problems before placing it. Here are some examples:

Not Legal	Legal
waiter	waitperson
salesman	salesperson
student	part-timer
young	eager
married couple	two-person team

Any type of word that mentions or implies a gender – should be changed. For example of an illegal ad, "Old fashioned secretary willing to wear a dress is wanted…" In addition, if that company's work place is made up of mainly women, that company is even more at risk for a lawsuit. Read Chapter Thirteen to learn about all the legal pitfalls and how to easily avoid them!

Advertise in Different Media

In addition to Internet job boards check out other media sources, radio stations, trade magazines, school bulletin boards, career centers, niche job boards, social media sites and billboards. Again, check out where your competition advertises and consider doing the same. If you're really short of employees and the Internet job boards are not producing anything, you should try the other media or rework the profile.

If you're using several media in your campaign, you should note where you're getting your best applicants because this information will be valuable for future campaigns.

Don't advertise in a media so far away from your area that you attract people who'll need to make a long commute. If a person has a forty-five minute commute or more, he will almost certainly look for work closer to home after he starts with you.

Ad Options

Consider paying extra for better placement on the job boards. Many offer premium spots or allow you to pay more per click to get your ad to the top of the list. Some ads may need to be reposted weekly to keep them at the top of a job seekers search.

How do You Want Applicants to Respond to Your Ad?

Applicants can respond by phone, career site, or by resume. Which way depends on what you want, and that decision should depend on the type of job. The initial contact for most career type jobs should be done through a resume sent by e-mail or uploaded to your career site. If you are using an applicant tracking system consider making it as easy as possible for applicant to apply and get their resume uploaded. Since the goal is usually to receive as many inquires as possible you want remove as many barriers as possible.

Since ads with a company name are more productive than ad's without company names you will inevitably get some phone calls and the occasional drop by. Usually these come when ad's are first posted. Prepare your administrators to handle these inquires professionally. I usually have a simple script, "Thank you for your interest in the open job position. Please respond to the job ad with a resume or by filling out our on line application. I can assure you we review every applicant to determine if they are possible fit. We will call you if we feel you meet our requirements to continue the interview process." Keep it simple repeat yourself if needed, and most people will get the hint. Even though this is annoying it is a necessary inconvenience to get the largest response possible. An exception is for an entry level position where you will receive a large number of applicants regardless of what you do. In these cases you may want to post an anonymous ad.

What to do Once you Begin to get Applicants

It is important to prepare to act quickly once you start receiving responses from your job ad. The best candidates are hot commodities, the only way to keep them around is get them engaged in the selection process as quickly as possible and keep it moving. I recommend setting aside a few hours 2 to 3 days a week to call you best applicants and conduct phone screens to start the process. Once you determine someone is a good potential fit for your job keep them moving through the process as quickly as possible. A good rule of thumb is move to the next step of the process within 48 hours of each contact.

Internet Hiring

Start by pretending you are looking for the job you intend to post. Google and search the major job boards for similar job titles and descriptions. This will give you an idea of which job ads are coming to the top, where you want to be. Since getting top search results change often do this each time you are preparing to post a requisition.

Some tips on designing your postings:

* Think up intriguing titles.
* Describe the job in the first 2 to 3 sentences.
* State the salary in those first few lines.
* Ask recent hires what key words they used to do their searches.
* Provide an easy and clear way for candidates to respond to your ads.
* Make online application forms short and easy.
* Focus on skills and opportunities, not requirements.
* Also, review my advertising section on the previous pages.
* Don't say too much about the job functions. Discuss the performance expectations instead of requirements.

Most Popular Job boards

Since you are looking for the largest response possible you should seriously consider posting your ad on multiple job boards. In order of popularity and effectiveness:

* Careerbuilder.com
* Monster.com
* Indeed.com
* LinkedIn
* Craigslist
* Ladders.com
* Facebook.com
* Niche or industry-specific job boards
* College job boards
* Local city job boards
* Technical school job boards

Other Sources
Some high schools have typing students on an apprenticeship program who'll work on a part-time basis for slightly above minimum wage.

The unemployment office has people looking for jobs, but I've never been able to establish how good they are.

Private technical schools have placement personnel looking for jobs for their upcoming graduates; this has also proven successful.

College job boards are good for finding interns or part-time workers who are very good.

You may be surprised at the number of sources available if you keep asking around. Ask your employees for the places or media they used when they were looking for a job.

Testing can Reduce the Negatives of some Types of Recruiting
If you use testing early in the selection process, especially skill and attitude testing, running an ad will be much less time-consuming and more accurate. Testing in this case saves interviewing time and finds faults more efficiently.

If you're using a recruiter as well as testing, you can more easily justify the twenty to thirty percent commission investment. Tests are good for pointing out hidden problems that interviewing may overlook. Don't let recruiters convince you that tests are unnecessary, and don't work with a recruiter who refuses to let you test their candidates. You will find that tests tend to force a recruiter into doing a good job.

Keep the Goal in Mind
Remember that it's not a matter of running one ad for two weeks and hiring the best of the bunch. The best of the bunch may be unsuitable. The campaign should continue as long as it takes to find the right person. I've seen it take two weeks or as long as a year, and the year involved recruiters. Finding the right person never takes a fixed amount of time.

A failure to find enough good people quickly enough is usually always caused by a lack of networking.

The next two chapters will give you some ideas on better ways of efficiently screening resumes and applicants.

Chapter 6

Effectively Screening Resumes

Resumes are one of those necessary evils that are difficult to do without. Evils, because reading through them and making up one's mind about piles of resumes can be stressful. This chapter is about reducing the time and stress it takes and increasing the efficiency of sorting through those piles of colored parchments.

Resumes

The word resume means a summary, so a resume is supposed to be a condensed version of a person's work history. However, most people write their resumes to show a wonderful and amazing description of their work experience and accomplishments. After reading through them, you start wondering why you were never lucky enough to have such great people working for you. Any one of them may be great.

Resumes come in three basic types:

* A resume gives a person's employment history in a time sequence with some detail of each job.
* A resume highlights a person's strengths, skills and knowledge without listing a job history.
* A resume is combination of the previous two.

The only resume to be concerned about is the second one; it may cover up frequent changes of employment due to the applicant's bad attitude or attempts to hide the fact he is a wolf.

Why do we even bother with Resumes?
The basic two purposes of resumes are for applicants to get interviews and for employers to eliminate applicants who are obviously not qualified. It helps give the employer some basic information on a candidate without a lot of questioning. It also helps reduce the number of applicants in an effective and easy way.

Evaluating a Resume
Although research has shown that thirty percent of resumes contain at least some false information, the bigger problem is the missing negatives. One common falsification is the missing job. When the applicants know they did poorly and had terrible relationships with bosses, they want that information as buried as possible. On the resumes, they might stretch out the duration of previous jobs, hoping you won't check into them. Don't believe everything you read.

If an expensive looking resume subliminally convinces you the person is a good candidate, it has successfully influenced you. Because you have been subliminally convinced, you won't realize where those good thoughts came from. Unless you are looking for a marketing person, do not let fancy resumes count any more than plain old black ink on white paper. All you are looking for in those resumes are reasons to eliminate those that do not fit one or more of the *must haves*. After reading a resume, you know nothing about the person's personality and therefore very little about the person.

You can usually establish what sort of work people have been doing by reading between the lines on a resume. How frequently they change employers is also usually obvious. You may be able to establish how long they have been doing certain functions, but it is difficult to determine their success.

Except for how frequently they change employers and unemployment gaps between employers, you have no way of knowing what sort of attitude they have or what degree of interest they may have in your opening. You may or may not be able to tell if they are still working, or if they have a history of long unemployment between employers, as they may have covered them up with generalized dates and falsehoods. The main value of a resume for an employer is how competent or experienced the applicant may be—**as a starting point.**

The best and most effective way to screen applicants is to check resumes against desired experiences, stability with employers, and to some degree—successes. In addition, the resumes may give other information, such as credentials and experience with certain equipment, software and languages.

The important red flags are moving from one company to another more than five times in a ten-year period, or the lengths of employment have become very short. You need to examine resumes closely to determine whether there have been excessive changes.

If you want super employees, do not procrastinate over checking out resumes. Employers who hire competent people with "hidden" bad attitudes do this because they are too slow. Let me explain. Competent wolves are willing to wait; good people get hired quickly. The perceptive employers will spot the good people and act faster than they normally do. Someone on the ball will have the best chance at them. Read resumes as soon as they arrive or have someone else do it. Do not let good people go to your competitors.

Mistakes

If you want super employees, you need more than just skills, education and experience. Lena Adil applied for the Vice-president of engineering at a large telecommunications company and was one of three finalists. They scheduled her to have a teleconferencing call at Kinko's because the company was on the other side of the country. However, up to this point, she had only talked to the recruiters, and the only information the employers knew about her was on her resume and the recruiter's sales presentation. Remember, recruiters are not experienced on personality, culture, and attitude. The company had narrowed the field without knowing anything about three big question marks—personality, cultural values, and attitude. This company made the same old mistake of thinking resumes and recruiters do most of the exposure. You cannot blame them for this because the emphasis on being qualified has been so overrated. That company would have had a better chance of finding a super team player by narrowing the field to about ten and having a short interview with each one.

Evaluating the Cover Letter

The real purpose of a resume and cover letter is to help you make a decision of who to call in for an interview. The cover letter may explain things the resume does not, especially as it may relate to the advertised position. Let's face it, the cover letter is just more razzel dazzle and that's how you should take it. However it will help you disqualify people who have poor communication skills. Look at the cover letters of your top candidates one more time going into the final interviews. They will mean a lot more to you once you know your candidate better. Ask them questions related to facts they state in their cover letters, make sure your candidate can explain them fully and with consistency

How to Manage this Pile of Paper Work?

This may seem like a lot work to screen 100 to 500 resumes and you are partially correct. If you have a good system and a plan this task can take 15 minutes a day. Review the resumes keeping the questions on your resume evaluation form in mind. Select all the resumes that seem to fit, no need to go through with a fine toothcomb here. Move those resumes to a file or print them out. Once you have selected the resumes you might be interested in go back through the potentials one more time. Look more carefully at each one using your evaluation form. Cherry pick the best ones and move them to a separate file or pile. Keep the other resumes as backup's, these should have some potential but not the best. You can sort through those later if your initial top picks don't work out. Once you have the best resumes sorted out then do initial contacts via e-mail to schedule short 20 minute phone screens. You can also get started right away and call these candidates, most of them will talk to you, this can save some time scheduling interviews that may results in a poor candidate.

The Resume Evaluation Form

After going through stack upon stack of resumes, you may start wondering what you are looking for. You may discard good people because you have lost your focus, or you may ask people in for interviews who are not qualified. Developing an evaluation form solves these problems and makes the review process easier. Two sample forms are given at the end of this chapter.

Another reason to use this form is to help you organize your thoughts. After going through a mountain of resumes, you may start wondering who did what. Nevertheless, if you have your forms filled in and stapled to the resumes, you know whom you are still interested in and what questions you need to ask. No more thinking needed.

In order to develop your own resume evaluation form, you need to look for the most common reasons for disqualification first, with the less common reasons last. For example, let's say you are looking for a desktop publishing expert and the most common missing skill for your business is being capable of handling a high volume desk. This attribute would be on the top of your list.

Developing the form involves looking at the profile covered in Chapter Four and deciding which two or three skills, experiences or qualifications the person must have. For this form, three is the maximum, two is best.

Now you should make up a form (see attached form for a sample), including a space at the top for their name. Under that, write down your questions from the previous paragraph, leaving an inch or two between each one for notes.

See the example resume evaluation form for the remaining questions. Stable job history, gaps in employment, and successful job history are details you can get from the resume. If this information is not available from the resume, you can leave it blank, letting you know the questions you still need to ask. When you talk to the candidate for the first time, all the relevant information and questions will be readily available. In addition, it is critical to ask the obvious about information already presented on the resume to determine the candidate's honesty and validity of their resume.

A stable job history would consist of applicants being with each employer three or more years in the last six to ten years. An applicant who has been with an employer ten or more years and currently still employed is likely to have a good attitude, but may have other problems—such as not enough ambition. These people may be great fits for positions offering little future change in roles.

An unstable job history would look something like this. The candidate has had a new employer about once a year throughout her career, or a new employer every two plus years but getting shorter and shorter. Several employer-changes in the last few years—no matter how good the reasons sound— are a big red flag.

Gaps in employment, current unemployment or both are signs of attitude problems. Unemployment for four or more months or current unemployment for more than four months is a big gap and a red flag. The candidate may have been employed and fired in that time and not noted it on the resume. Good employees are in demand and seldom have gaps in employment.

The question "successful job history" is there to help remind you to note down any accomplishments the candidates have included. Are they still getting better? Have they leveled out? Are they getting worse? You can check this by seeing what they have accomplished in each position and how often they have been promoted. For example, a salesperson's resume may state they always made their quotas. Remember this may or may not be true and the quotas may have been easy. However, it gives us hope and is worth checking into.

More explanations and suggestions on this subject are offered in the next chapter.

How to Deal with Resumes Using the Form

The first thing to do is to skim through the resume. Look for obvious information that would disqualify the applicant. Do not be concerned if the applicant has failed to send in a cover letter or anything else that you requested in the ad. If the resume and cover letter indicate a possible fit, start filling in the resume evaluation form.

The next thing to do to is to put the person's name on the form. Answer the first five questions as completely as possible. If the answer is an obvious yes, put yes. If you are not sure of an answer, write out the best answer you can. Now you know what you need to ask the applicant. You also know who to forget and who to pursue. If you have doubts about someone, include them in the pursue pile—because it is only a resume, there is little to lose and a lot to gain.

Is the Form worth it?

That form is your lifeboat when you are reading through that sea of resumes. It helps remind you to be looking for those five or six main requirements for a super employee. Rather than get caught up with the glowing achievements, you will be able to focus better. And when you have your pile of filled in forms, you know exactly what to ask the candidates the first time you start interviewing them. You will not need to struggle looking through the resume trying to figure out what to ask. Most important of all, you are less likely to miss the important requirements you want.

SAMPLE RESUME EVALUATION FORM FOR A MANAGER

Applicant's Name: _____

Has the applicant managed employees for over two years?

Has the applicant managed more than three people at one time?

Has the applicant used software related to your industry for a minimum of one year? (This is a sample only and not a typical requirement for a manager, each position would have its own specific requirements)

Does the applicant have a stable job history? (If jobs not listed chronologically, what is candidate hiding?)

Are there any gaps between jobs?

Does the applicant have a successful job history?

(You can ask the following questions over the phone. See the next chapter regarding that interview.)

What are the main activities you have done for a living?

Which places would you rather live and which places would you rather not live and why? (An employer asking someone to move to a cold climate might ask this question. Each position may have its own specific concerns. For example, sound levels, smells, overtime and so on).

What are you looking for in your next job?

Why did you leave your last position? Or why are you planning to leave your current position?

(On this line, write down the concerns the employer usually has keeping this position filled. Write out a question to detect the concern.)

Comments about the applicant:

Applicant's Name: _____
(List job requirements that you can check on a resume.)

Chapter 7

Questions for Your First Phone Contact

Have you ever looked over a resume, decided this person is qualified, arranged for the person to come in for an interview, and within a few minutes realized the person is not who you expected? You then have the problem of having to nicely end the interview. By the time the ordeal is over, you went out of your way to set up an appointment, wasted time interviewing, and put yourself in a difficult position. There is a better way to interview applicants to avoid this type of situation, yet still find those super candidates.

If you read and liked the idea of using the Resume Evaluation Form in the last chapter, this next idea will fit into your screening program like a foot into a comfortable shoe. It involves calling candidates and asking them for information that is missing from their resumes.

The purpose of this first call is to either find the qualified or to gently let down the unqualified. It usually only takes ten to twenty minutes to determine if the person will have a chance. If you like what you hear, you can set a time for them to come in and get interviewed. If you don't like what you hear, all you need to do is remind them you only called to get more information and that you now have it. From my experience, most people accept the gentle let down without a battle.

The Resume Evaluation Form

Call the person if you like the information on the Resume Evaluation Form. Call as many applicants as you can that still have possibilities—as you still don't have a clue which one really is qualified. Resume information is not that complete or reliable. And if the resume failed to give much information, it is still a good idea to call. Once again this game is about casting the widest net, so take advantage of short phone screens to determine who might be a good fit.

Use the sample resume evaluation form at the end of the last chapter during the phone interview. The first few questions should specifically address skills and experiences needed for the position.

The answer to *What are the main activities you've done for a living?* gives you an insight into their major skills and abilities. Their answers should be close to the important experiences you're looking for.

The next question is a question you make up yourself. The purpose of this question is to make sure the applicant will not have a problem with the job after being hired. For example, the job often requires overtime, which has caused many a good employee to quit. For this example, you could design a question about what they like and dislike about working overtime. Ask the question so that your concern in not apparent. (See Chapters Nine and Ten.)

This question covers these concerns:

* Work conditions (shared offices, underground work areas, under houses)
* Travel (number of days a week likely to be away from home)
* Overtime (amount of average overtime per month)
* Risks (working on the outside of a high-rise building)
* Environments (hot or cold)
* Frequent relocation (need to move one's home regularly)
* Knowledge (needs to learn a language, culture or geography)
* Job activity (making cold calls, presentations in front of groups and other scary activities)

The answer to *What are you looking for in your next job?* gives you an idea of the person's interest and tells how long they are likely to remain with you.

Why did you leave your last position? Or *Why are you planning to leave your current position?* gives information about their good or poor attitude reasons for leaving the last job. It also gives you information about their current working status. Because most candidates have a well worked out answer to this question, I suggest probing their responses.

Short Phone Interview

Call the applicant and leave a message if she is not there. Leave this information:

* Your name.
* Your number.
* A good time for them to reach you.
* What the ad was about in one short sentence.
* A message that you have questions about their resume.

Place the Resume Evaluation Form in a handy place, so you can easily ask her your questions without forgetting the main points.

As you talk to the applicant, ask all the questions on the form you didn't answer "yes" to when you checked her resume. Write down her answers as she talks and keep this interview less than twenty minutes. Don't ask for the applicant's questions, although you should answer questions without indicating what is important to you or what profile you're hoping to find.

Forms are useful time savers for documenting interviews. Taking notes makes it easier to review pros and cons when it is difficult to decide if you want the person to come in or not. Notes can also be useful a year later for following up on those who were hired. Notes are a reality check of how accurately the manager read the candidates.

You can eliminate those applicants who don't do well in the phone interview. Tell them you have all the information that you need. If the applicant's answers look good, ask them to come in for an interview. Use the face-to-face or scheduled phone interviews to explore the details. The purpose of the short phone interview is to decide if the person is worth pursuing.

Testing

If the person did well on the short phone interview, you may want him tested as the next step. E-mail him the questionnaires and have them marked before you schedule the next meeting. Don't use testing as a screening tool as it can cause legal problems. Another short interview can eliminate someone who did poorly on your tests.

Great Value—Small Investment

This simple, short phone call has many values. It not only saves emotional awkwardness and stress; it also opens the gates for those people who may not look good on paper but turn out better in person.

Chapter 8

An Effective System to Handle the Paperwork

Whether it is for a legal or a discovery reason, make good use of the forms you have applicants fill in. Although paperwork is a boring subject, the purpose of this chapter is to show you how to organize the process to reduce interview time and make better decisions.

There is Gold in That Application Form

All applicants should fill in an application form before the first one-on-one interview with no exceptions. These forms not only give you basic information about the person but also give you some subtle insights into the person. For example, their hobbies, interests, and what they studied at school may not be in alignment with what the job is all about. The application form also helps get some written approval to check into certain areas of an applicant's life. For example, you need a written Okay from the applicant to do a reference check for a current position.

Look at the reasons they give for leaving their past three or four jobs. If they were fired, consider that a strong indicator of a bad attitude. The "Lied to" reason for leaving is likely to be a negative attitude indicator, but it may depend how they were lied to. "Laid off" is considered more negative than positive and requires more investigation. "Quit for higher salary" is also another possible negative attitude indicator. "Quit for a bigger challenge" is acceptable if the person went directly to another job. "Quit because of a long commute" is acceptable.

Make sure to ask them to complete the form in its entirety including past jobs over 10 years. Watch for how thoroughly a candidate and completed the application form. Make sure to ask them to complete the form in its entirety including past jobs from over 10 years ago

You can purchase these employment application forms at stationery stores and online since the laws change regularly, don't use outdated ones.

You should also consider using applicant tracking systems, there are numerous low cost cloud based programs available now. I would encourage you to choose a system that has a very easy and basic process for completing an application. Make sure the system can easily and accurately sparse resume data into your forms, this will keep your applicants and you more engaged in the process. You can always have your more qualified candidates go back and enter more detailed information prior to the first in person interview.

The Best Way to Test Applicants

Assessments and testing are best done after the first in-person or phone interview. Whenever a person sounds good on the short phone interview, have the applicants complete the assessment prior to scheduling an in person interview. If you do wait to test your applicants immediately following the first in person interview can help you save time having the candidate return to take the assessments. Well practiced interviewers can wait until later rounds to use assessments to compare two or more highly qualified candidates.

Test the applicants at the office if at all possible. The only exception is having applicants complete the assessments prior to the first in person interview. Ideally have applicants complete skill tests early in the process then give more in depth assessments in later rounds of interviews. Following these steps will save you many hours with a poor candidate and emotional attachment to bad applicant.

How to take a Test Takers Complaints to Advantage

A very small percentage of people will complain about filling in tests. This tends to confirm that they are critical and uncooperative. Use their reactions to testing as an indicator of future cooperativeness. Train your assistant to write any job seeker comments down so you can add it to the applicant's paperwork.

Competency Tests

Give competency tests to uncover skill levels, such as typing accuracy with details, problem solving, or filing. The results of competency tests are valuable, so testing should be done where applicable. The best time to give these tests is prior to the first in-person interview. If the applicant can't perform tasks that require basic skills related to the job they probably are not worth your time to interview.

How Assistants can Help

Before the applicants come in for testing, you need to brief the receptionist and your assistant on what you want them to do. Testing packages and application forms need to be prepared in the sequence you want them filled in. You also need to set aside a desk or table or at least a clipboard and pencil for the applicants.

When the applicants come in, you or your assistant should do the following:

* Offer them some refreshments.
* Route them to the computer and give them the application and testing instructions.
* Tell them the assessments also measure how honestly they are filled in. (Only necessary if the assessments do that like mine do.)

After the applicant has filled in all the tests, assessments, and application forms, you or the assistant should tell the applicant to wait or take a seat in reception. The interviewer should look over the results and completed forms and then have the applicant come into his office for the first day's interview.

If you have an assistant and you like this procedure, all you need to do is have him read this chapter and apply it.

Legal Forms

All the legal forms and the written employment agreement (if there is one) need to be filled in and signed before the person starts work. Don't let her start before this is done under the name of expediency.

Let Paperwork be Your Friend

This procedure has been tested hundreds of times with success. It is organized in a way to get information to the interviewer in a timely manner. If an applicant gets upset with it, you maybe uncovering cooperation issues. Paperwork is not that glamorous, but it can save you time and improve your end result.

Chapter 9

The Key Stumbling Blocks to Good Interviewing—Exposed

If you have ever been fooled by a job applicant (and who hasn't?), this chapter will tell you why you were fooled and what you can do about it.

Applicants use experts in the hiring field to coach and instruct them on how to appear better than reality. They learn how to answer the most common interview questions in a way to fool most interviewers. Even when you ask applicants difficult questions, they can come back with good responses. For example, if you ask applicants why they were fired from their last jobs, they may say the managers had asked them to do something unethical and they had refused to do it. Unfortunately, you'll only get their side of the story.

To make matters worse for interviewers, the terrible applicants go from job to job and are interviewed many times, getting lots of practice at honing their skills at looking good.

Many books are written and courses are given on how to get a job. Unfortunately, these experts and books focus on taking advantage of the interviewer's weaknesses. The applicants are trained to please interviewers—not necessarily to be honest. Some of the ideas taught to applicants include:

* Manipulate the interviewer into doing most of the talking.
* Do not answer the interviewer's questions as he intends. Instead, use the questions as a means of changing the subject to what you want to say.
* Give well-prepared, good-sounding answers.

Now the interviewer can arm himself or herself against the tactics of unqualified applicants trying to get a job.

You are not Looking for the Perfect Candidate

The first thing to understand is what you are trying to do by interviewing. Like testing and reference checking, you interview candidates to see if they fit your profile. It is better to look for a candidate's departures from the profile, the applicant's flaws, than how good they are. A resume will tell you what they say are their strengths. All the interviewer should focus on is uncovering the flaws.

If they have several flaws or a major flaw, you should turn the applicant down for the job. You need to interview a candidate until you are certain the candidate fits the profile or the opposite—has too many flaws, a major flaw, or does not fit the profile you need.

"Several flaws" would describe a candidate having multiple borderline traits under the *Must Have* or *Absolutely Not* profile categories (see Chapter Four). A "major flaw" would be one definite missing *Must Have* trait or the existence of a definite *Absolutely Not* trait. For example, a candidate who is very shy but is well-organized, smart, and has all other traits required for a salesperson should be turned down if "shy" is under the *Absolutely Not* category.

Don't focus on the exceptionally good traits, as there is a tendency to overlook a major flaw. The exception is the compulsive strength that is the cause of another weakness. For example, a salesperson that talks effectively but can't shut up will never be able to listen. By "can't shut up," I mean talking over everything the interviewer says as well.

If the resume looks acceptable, you're better off checking for flaws first. When you find someone with no major flaws or few flaws, you'll have a super candidate. With this said, the focus of this chapter will be to uncover flaws.

Definite Flaws

You know you have a definite flaw when it keeps coming up in tests, interviews, and reference checks. If a flaw comes up once, you note it and question it without showing you are concerned about it. For example, when a candidate admits not being able to ask for help, you could say, "That is common, tell me more about that." If it comes up several times, you can count on it being a definite concern.

You can also confirm flaws by thinking about how the flaw explains other behavior the applicant may have mentioned. For example, you suspect the candidate is not motivated and you think about the questions he asked you about vacation times and how flexible you were on allowing time off. You also remember how much he talked to you about golf when the interview first got started. A good pre-employment test would also show this motivation problem.

An interviewer's opinion or gut feeling is not sufficient. The interviewer should have strong evidence before deciding the applicant has a suitable or unsuitable profile. The interviewer should know exactly what are all the applicant's strengths and weaknesses and why she or he knows it.

Someone who fits the profile will meet each of the following queries:

1. Does the candidate have all the skills to do the work?
2. Does the candidate have the education to do the work?
3. Does the candidate have the experience to do the work?
4. Is the candidate bright enough, quick enough, creative enough?
5. Will the candidate be satisfied with the amount of money and benefits the company can afford to pay?
6. Does the candidate have a good nature (hard worker, positive, responsible, truthful, loyal and supportive)?

7. Will the candidate fit into the culture of the company?
8. Does the candidate have the right personality for the work?
9. Does the candidate have the interest in doing the work?
10. Does the candidate like working inside (desk jockey) or outside?
11. Will the candidate be able to meet the company's attendance requirements?
12. Does the candidate have the ability to perform specific job functions, with or without special accommodation? (See Americans with Disabilities Act in the chapter on legal questioning).

Common Interviewer Faults

These are the four common interview faults:

* Talking too much. (Explaining, not interviewing.)
* Emotionally believing one has found the perfect candidate before completing all the interviews, testing and reference checks.
* Jumping to conclusions from scraps of information.
* Carelessly divulging to the candidate what the interviewer hopes to hear.

Talking too Much

The purpose of interviewing is to find the applicant's faults. How can you do that when you're the one doing the talking? Also, you can be easily manipulated if you're talking too much. When interviewers are talking about what they have done and what they are doing, the person listening is stroking their ego. So talking too many a waste time and opens the interviewer up to being manipulated.

Another fault with talking is the tendency to turn candidates off from wanting the job as they hear things they don't like. On the other hand, when you question, you're inferring you have a great job to offer without directly saying it. If the candidate can get you talking about your favorite ideas, you're much more likely to be sold on the candidate. My clients and I have come up with the saying: "THE PERSON DOING THE TALKING IS THE ONE BEING SOLD." If you, the interviewer, are doing the talking, then you will tend to be sold on the applicant, regardless of their qualifications. When the candidates talk, they want the job more and more as they talk and talk. I know it sounds unbelievable, but notice how your feelings for candidates change depending on who did the talking. Also, rather than give a long speech on how great your company is, just give a short summary that does not expose the profile you're looking for. The more you question and listen, the more you'll find out, and the more you'll know about the appropriateness of the candidate.

I have something to confess. When my friends and acquaintances ask for advice on getting a job, it is very simple. I just say to them to get the interviewer talking and I even give them a list of questions to ask. They mostly come back and tell me they were offered the job. They are amazed that the interviewer did almost all the talking and found out very little about them! I once belonged to a job connection group and one piece of advice they gave was to turn the interview into a conversation by asking questions. And some hiring websites list the questions applicants should ask to get the interviewer talking.

Emotionally Believing You've Found the Perfect Candidate

If you feel you have the perfect candidate before thoroughly testing, interviewing and reference checking, you're making a mistake. It is human nature to make this faux pas so don't feel bad about it. The problem with this interview fault is the difficulty to see or hear anything negative after you have fallen in love. You know the person will be perfect, so why bother checking out the person anymore? For example, let's say you are sold on a receptionist applicant, but she tells you about a problem of arriving on time. The smitten interviewer sees this honesty as a plus even though arriving late, on this position, is a reason for termination in the company. Realize that when you fall in love; you are blinded.

I know a company that fell into this one big time. The management team needed a Sales Manager badly. As "luck" would have it, Allen Shields (made up name) had been selling to the company as equipment Sales Manager. Allen had impressed the management team with his sales ability and wanted to work for these managers as their National Sale Manager savior. The managers interviewed and tested him in a half-hearted manner because they already "knew" he was good. The pre-employment test results indicated some attitude problems, but they dismissed them as, "All sales people are like that." During the honeymoon period, as they flew him from office to office, the effort to explain to Allen what was needed became a bigger and bigger chore. He just didn't seem to be getting it. He wanted to do things his own way and be promoted to Vice President of Sales by the end of the first month. One slight problem was that he upset the senior managers with his selfish agenda. Finally, after paying him a big salary and a lot of travel expenses with no results, they had to let him go because he just didn't fit in. He had a bad attitude.

When you feel like you have a perfect candidate, think about all those other times you felt the same way, but the person turned out poorly. Always check off each one of the twelve queries (previously mentioned in this chapter) with diligence, and only when you are sure of each one should you fall in love.

Jumping to Conclusions from Scraps of Information

It is human nature to make decisions quickly because we no longer have to bother with the "unknown." Refraining from making decisions is unnatural, difficult and time consuming—but worth it.

Avoid making generalized judgments of people. Learn to keep questioning people even though you think you know the answers. Ask questions about what they are saying even though you think you already know. I hope you get the point. It is not easy.

Interviewers typically form opinions about a person at first sight. They also form opinions too quickly after applicants tell them of the success they'll bring to their company. Bad ones will prey on the interviewer's or supervisor's greed. It's an old trick but unfortunately it works. Managers and interviewers want to believe the candidate will be great. However, in order to improve on this fault of not jumping to conclusions, interviewers have to keep convincing themselves they don't know how good the applicant is until all the interview questions have been answered and analyzed, test results have been examined, and reference checks have been completed.

If a new interviewer *really* understands what I am writing about, he has my respect. I had to learn the hard way. Early in my career, after I had been thoroughly impressed by the answers of a few different applicants, who turned out to be complete misfits, I realized I didn't know the truth until I had turned over *all* the rocks.

Inadvertently Divulging to the Candidate What the Interviewer Hopes to Hear

Inadvertently communicating what you hope a candidate will say to you is a huge subject in the interview process. Skill in this area makes the most difference between the expert and the ineffective interviewer. In fact, interviewers can't detect attitude issues unless they overcome this very common mistake.

Carelessly divulging your hopes is the act of letting the candidate know what you want them to say so they can effectively reduce your concerns or side step the truth. For example, the interviewer asks, "Are you a good team player?" and the applicant replies, "Of course I am!" The positive answer is the only answer unless the person doesn't want the job. Now the candidate knows that "being a good team player" is important to the interviewer and will make sure she convinces him of that. Even a subtle question like, "Do you prefer to be on time or be late?" clearly shows the candidate that lateness is a big no-no in the company.

In some ways it is another form of talking too much. The worst mistake is explaining the type of person you're looking for. The candidate can't help but become the ideal. If you tell the candidates you're looking for an honest, high-energy, aggressive person, they will tell you they are exactly that. Some will not only say they are but will attempt to convince you of that. At some level, everyone thinks they are honest, energetic and aggressive, so it's easy to say so. The biggest problem with this common fault is the interviewer's belief in the candidate's response, without realizing how easy it was for the candidate to know what to say. If you want to skip over this stumbling block, I don't blame you. The good news is that if you ask questions from the interview questions in Chapter Eleven, you won't make this mistake as often.

Good interview questions are easy to ask but are only part of the answer. You also need to ask about answers without showing your hand. The best way to do this is to focus on finding out more, rather than trying to manipulate. Manipulation can backfire and give away your hand. Let's say Scott responds to your question of why he left the previous job by saying he left for a bigger challenge, now to ask him about his answer. A bad question would be, "Were you bored at that job?" It is bad because the candidate now needs to sell you on why it was not boring at all, and he had never been bored in his life. Instead, just ask to find out more. A good question may be, "Scott, what was wrong with the challenge on that previous job?" It is a good question because you haven't communicated what you are concerned about.

Another way to avoid this problem is to ask broad questions around the subject you are concerned about. Let's take for example you are interviewing an applicant applying for a supervisor position, but you are concerned about this person's actual ability to supervise people. You could ask for likes and dislikes about supervising. The candidate doesn't have a clue what you want. The likes and dislikes answers will confirm what you wanted to check. On the other hand, if you asked, "Do you micro manage your people?" you might be told, "Of course I don't." The answer sounds convincing, but actually means nothing because it is obvious what you wanted to hear. If you believe the answer is true, you start building up this false picture of the person (See chapter ten, Getting to the Truth, for how to ask second and third questions).

Semi-specific questions also give away the profile causing the candidate's answers to mislead the interviewer. For example, a question asking if a supervisor applicant would prefer dealing with employees' concerns or dealing with discipline is still communicating what you want to hear. The person's answer will most likely be one of loving all parts of the job. That answer tells you nothing and has alerted the applicant to convince you how much she loves confronting emotional issues. A better question may be to ask *how* she goes about dealing with employee concerns. By emphasizing *how*, the candidate doesn't know what you're looking for. Sure, she will figure that dealing with concerns is important, but she doesn't know if you want her to confront people or sympathize with them.

The interviewer's body language, like raising an eyebrow, can communicate approval or disapproval. Applicants can read body language and match their presentation to it. For example, after asking Valerie a bunch of questions she suddenly says, "I get so annoyed with customers that I swear at them." The interviewer, who hadn't been writing anything, immediately writes this down. Valerie notices and says, "Oh, I only swear under my breath. The customer would never know it." A poker face and delayed writing is the best approach to interviewing.

As tempting as it is for new interviewers, asking directly for faults will not give you what you want. Candidates may know some of their more obvious faults, like a criminal record, which they are unlikely to volunteer anyway. They may not be aware of other faults due to their own self-denial and their own mixed up idea of the employer's ideal profile. Asking for faults in a more general way, such as, "What are your faults" will not give away the profile; however, the candidate's answers will not be very meaningful. Asking about a specific fault will give the profile away and is not recommended. But there is a good way of finding faults.

We know that a great strength can be a great weakness. We know that candidates like to talk about their strengths. In fact, they are taught in "interviewee school" to do just that. Let me point out how asking about a strength can be revealing. When strengths show up from tests or other sources, you can tell candidates those observations and ask them to elaborate. As long as the candidate doesn't know what you're looking for, you are not communicating what you want. This does take a little skill to pull off successfully. For example, the test showed a talking compulsion. You could say, "The test results showed that you are strong communicator. We like that in our salespeople. Tell me about your talking ability." This might look like you are communicating a trait, but the candidate doesn't know your real concerns. You could also observe the talking trait in the interview, especially if you can't get a word in edgeways. The reason you want to explore their strengths is to learn if the strengths are compulsive thus causing other problems. A strength is almost always off set by a weakness either big or small. As long as the candidates don't know what your real concerns are you're interviewing effectively.

If you follow the questions in the interview question, chapter eleven, they are designed to hide what is wanted by the interviewer. Then all you need to work on is getting good at the follow up questions.

To overcome this interviewer fault, focus on finding out more, rather than trying to manipulate. Ask open-ended questions (ones that ask for more information, rather than just yes or no answers) and stick to a set of good interview questions that don't show your hand.

Correcting this stumbling block, just like the other three, looks challenging. The good news is that with practice you will become a great interviewer. Also, some people don't always understand what you're communicating when you blow it—thank goodness. Know these common faults well so that you are very aware of them. Study them before every interview until it becomes a natural way of interviewing.

Interviewing Tips

Opening the Interview
Before starting an interview, you must make sure you won't be interrupted. Interruptions can be insulting, may lower respect and therefore restrict the applicant's openness.

The seating arrangement should be the most comfortable one for you. A relaxed attitude promotes more and better information from the candidate. Telling your name and title clears up any doubt or any nagging questions about you. Offering water, coffee or tea is a nice way of putting the candidate at ease. Good small talk subjects include the weather, the office, where they just drove from, or a common interest you may have noticed on an application form or resume. Small talk should only take a few minutes.

Take Notes

Notes are valuable during and after an interview. During an interview, notes can be used to keep track of where you are and to reference specific points. After the interview, the notes can help you list the pros and cons. The lists of pros and cons help you get a more objective look at the person. In the interview, most of us get a little mesmerized by the applicant, so lists of pros and cons wake us up. Notes can also help remind you of candidates you have interviewed, help as a training tool when you compare their answers to how they turned out in reality, and help protect you in case of legal problems.

In order to be able to make the lists, you should write down only pertinent and relevant information. Jot down the crux of information that confirms the profile you're looking for or departs from the profile. Also, noting how they say something or how slow they are to respond can be very relevant. About half a page to a page an hour is usually enough. Be careful to avoid writing down illegal knowledge such as age, place of birth, religion or marital status, even if volunteered.

Note major negatives more discreetly. Wait until the applicant answers the next question before you note the previous major negative. This action makes the candidate feel safer about telling you negatives. The worst response you could make to a negative statement would be one of shock, dismay, surprise, or anger and then immediately write it down. The neutral response is the best.

Indicators

Listen carefully to what candidates have on their mind. For example, a bad attitude indicator would be a candidate who comes back to his favorite sport a little too much. This candidate will be an employee more preoccupied with sports than with work. The following is a list of some attitude indicators and what they mean:

* A person who brings up stress a few times = bad attitude indicator
* A person who seems too focused on sports = bad attitude indicator

* A person overly concerned about money = bad attitude indicator
* A person overly interested in personal benefits = bad attitude indicator
* A person curious about company products = good attitude indicator
* A person interested in the company's research direction = good attitude indicator
* A person concerned about job security = bad attitude indicator
* A person willing to admit personal faults = good attitude indicator
* A person with no personal faults = bad attitude indicator
* A person making derogatory comments about a previous employer = bad attitude indicator

The bad attitude indicators can also be beliefs that are rigid or intolerant for certain situations. For example, "I hate it if employees are even one minute late" sounds good, as employees shouldn't be late, but the intolerance indicates excessive fault finding.

Indicators can come in several categories: very good, good, okay, bad, very bad or terrible. Saying they hate something is a worse indicator than a mere dislike of something. A description of a previous supervisor as an "idiot" indicates more of an attitude problem than describing someone as hard to get along with. Just to be clear, it is the candidate who has the attitude problem, not the previous supervisor. The *degree* of criticism is important and should be given more weight on the pros and cons list. Some bad indicators can be so strong you should end the interview as fast as diplomatically possible. For example, when a candidate is *proud* of a fault or offensive behavior, such as lying to bosses and getting away with it, you should end the interview.

The Winning Communication Style

In order to be a good interviewer, you must have the ability to communicate effectively. You don't need to be an extrovert, an entertainer, or a social butterfly. It's better to be a good questioner and listener because you need to be able to control the conversation while maintaining good rapport.

Control means directing the conversation where you want it to go and getting your questions answered, even if it means repeating them, but you don't need to be a manipulator.

You need good rapport and respect so that the person feels comfortable about telling you the vital information you need. This is done by asking open-ended questions. Open-ended questions ask for explanations rather than a "yes" or "no" answer. For example, you may ask which subjects they did well at during high school. When they tell you some, you may ask why they think they did so well in those subjects. As you listen, encourage them to talk. To actively listen, you may even repeat their answer with another question. For example, the interviewer says and asks, "Math and English. Those two subjects require two different personalities don't they?" If you try to control the conversation too much, they'll tend to be careful, and they're not likely to open up to you.

Good interviewers would appear to candidates as if they were just having a casual conversation at the water cooler. However, below that casual appearance the interviewer is deadly serious about finding out what the candidate is really all about. This casual approach makes the candidate feel like it is okay to say anything.

Interview Presentation

Don't give the impression you're critical, serious, or upset about anything the applicant may say. You should be playing down negative statements. For example, the candidate says, "My last boss was a tyrant," and the interviewer could wisely say, "I think almost everyone has had a boss like that. What happened in your case?" If anything, sound agreeable without communicating your concern. When interviewing, it's not your job to straighten out their ideas. Your job is to encourage them to talk as honestly as possible, find out what flaws they have and how bad the flaws are. Sounding friendly and agreeable, while being truthful, does this. Lying to candidates in the interview may work well, but could cause problems later.

Lengths of Interviews

Research has shown that about twenty minutes of interviewing takes place before interviewers change their first impression of a candidate. Research also shows the optimum return on time invested in an interview is between forty-five and sixty minutes. The length of an interview is also determined by the importance of the position and the salary of the candidate. For instance, a blue-collar or entry-level applicant interview may take about sixty minutes, while a president applicant may take sixteen hours or more over many interviews.

With a more responsible position, the interview should cover the last fifteen to twenty years of the candidate's career. With a less responsible position, the interview may only cover the last two jobs the person held.

If you're interviewing people who are applying for less responsible positions and have held six or more jobs, you should spend only five minutes on why they left those first positions and spend more time and different questions on the recent jobs.

Chronological Interviewing

This chronological style of interviewing does not have set questions to ask. You have the person tell you about their career from beginning to end while interjecting questions from time to time. But if you prefer this style, you will need to have mastered the principles in this and the next chapter. I recommend this style when interviewing senior executive type people followed by the sets of questions in Chapter Eleven.

The conduct on the most recent jobs is the best predictor of immediate future conduct. However, without understanding how the person got there won't make the answers on the recent jobs as meaningful.

By interviewing this way, you gain a greater understanding of the applicants. You learn how they have progressed and why. The candidates feel more open about early jobs because they feel they can excuse their faults as mistakes that happened a long time ago. This helps set the mood for recent jobs.

Note: The best predictor of future conduct comes from close examination of past conduct. More recent conduct is a more reliable predictor of future conduct. Basic behaviors seldom change. Therefore, get specific details of what the candidate actually did.

On the other hand, this style rarely shows up attitude indicators, which are better flushed out by "what if" type situations. With attitude, you are just trying to establish a person's current core values. The present way of thinking about things is more important than past descriptions of attitude behavior. This is mainly because people with bad attitudes avoid admitting to bad behavior.

Most importantly, in chronological interviewing, you're trying to understand the sequence of events, changes in an applicant's life, and the reason for these changes. Do this by asking about jobs in the sequence they were held with the following types of questions: "And then what happened?" or "What caused that?" and "Why?" Try to make sense of why the changes took place by digging deeper than the person was prepared for.

Good General Questions

On chronological questioning, fruitful areas are specific successes and accomplishments. One success should be examined for most jobs held, especially if an applicant's competency is in question. It is not that you are focusing on the applicant's strengths so much as the lack of accomplishments or the size of the successes.

You can discover interest and personality by asking these types of questions: "Which jobs did you enjoy the most?" and "What part of that job did you enjoy the most?"

Liking the Candidate

An interviewer's emotional likes or dislikes of an applicant are not good ways to judge. I have many clients who really liked people in an interview who later turned out to be unsuitable employees. Making hiring decisions based on emotion has never been a profitable way to do business.

Feeling Uncomfortable with an Applicant

We don't like people who threaten our comfort zones. We will make up "good reasons" to reject them, such as offering them low pay and then saying the candidates argued about it. A more common example may be the manager who is unconsciously looking for a weak individual. In this way, the manager can avoid different viewpoints or more successful ideas, which could be perceived as threats to her job security. Tests are very useful for an objective evaluation.

However, a candidate who still makes you feel uncomfortable after 60 minutes of interviewing may be too critical or have some other bad attitude trait. Because research has indicated it can take from 20 minutes to an hour to change a false first impression, it pays to keep interviewing until something tangible changes your mind. Regardless of the above, don't hire someone you don't like.

Strengths and Weaknesses

Asking about strengths and weaknesses has little value, except you may bring out the attitude indicator that the candidate can't think of anything he can improve. Most interviewers ask these questions but candidates have learned to sidestep meaningful answers. They know it is not good to say they have no weaknesses, so they make up a couple of innocent faults to satisfy the requirement. If you do decide to ask about that, start with strengths, as this establishes a comfortable way for the candidate to tell you weaknesses. But don't hold your breath.

A better approach is to ask what they think their supervisor would say were their strengths and weaknesses at the time. In this way, you get a better feel for the candidate. These questions are covered in Chapter Eleven on interview questions. The answers will be more honest if you make sure the applicant feels you will be checking all references.

When a weakness does come up, it's very important to keep that poker face. And never try to straighten them out in an interview about something they believe. What you say will not change their way of thinking—even though they may try to make you believe it. Instead, note it down as something negative. Always appear upbeat and unaffected by whatever they say. When they leave the interview, they shouldn't know what you think about them.

Research shows that candidates don't know the extent of their strengths and weaknesses. Some applicants feel that certain traits they have are strengths when in fact they are not. Some of course will exaggerate their abilities. You should never take a candidate's opinion of herself as the truth, but only as something to investigate further.

Another interesting piece of research I've done is following up on how these volunteered faults and weaknesses turned out in reality. Out of hundreds of interviews, only one volunteered fault actually turned out to be a fault that caused problems. More significant were those candidates who didn't volunteer any faults, as they seemed to have the most faults in reality. You are better off finding faults indirectly during the course of an interview.

The true value of direct strength and weakness questioning is learning more about a candidate's general personality. From strengths you may learn about compulsions and from weaknesses you may learn about degrees of denial. Don't ever think that just because a candidate sounds honest they have told you significant faults. Don't waste too much valuable interview time asking for strengths and weaknesses.

Salespeople

Before you hire salespeople who claim to have been successful, insist they bring you a copy of their tax statements for the last few years. In the United States, the tax statements will be 1099s or W2s. Experience has shown that about twenty-five percent of these applicants will never show up again because they exaggerated their success.

One wise sales manager would let salespeople brag about their numbers as he wrote them down. Then later in the interview he asked how much commission they got on each deal. Then he would ask if they could produce 1099s or W2s (the candidates now knew they may have to). Then he would ask how much they made per year during the times they were bragging about. He would then do some simple math. Sooner or later reality would unfold. He covered competency, personality, and honesty in one fell swoop.

Pregnant Pause

The pregnant pause is an extended length of time between the question and the answer. When a pregnant pause occurs, you should wait for the answer. Don't break the silence, don't offer an answer or try to change the question. Refrain from helping the poor candidate out. I know that sounds cruel, but when you do help you miss opportunities to learn valuable insights into the person. Don't lose sight of the objective.

Expect pregnant pauses when you ask for specific examples. You may have to encourage applicants to keep looking for answers to your questions. Tell them you have plenty of time so they can have a chance to remember something significant. If they can't find an answer, tell them you will come back later to the question and then return to it. I am often surprised how often they will think of an answer unexpectedly.

Candidates Questions

There is a value in candidates asking you questions. What they ask tells you what they are thinking. For example, "How much does the job pay?" asked too early on tells you their focus is heavily on themselves. Especially since most people know that. It indicates a what's-in-it-for-me attitude problem or in plain English—selfish. An example of a positive question could be "What's being done to sell that product in the international markets?" This question focuses on the employer. See indicators earlier in this chapter for more examples.

On the other hand, there are two liabilities in answering a candidate's questions:

* You may give away an exact description of who you are looking for before you decide you want to make the candidate an offer.
* You may start talking and become overly sold on the candidate. As covered earlier, the one who is talking is usually the one being sold.

Selling the Applicant

You sell applicants on the job mainly by asking good questions. This subliminally communicates that the company is top-of-the-line. In general, the more the applicants talk, the more interested they become in the position offered.

Explore what the person wants and show him how he can have that by working for your company. This should take a minor percentage of the interview time or in many cases, practically no time at all. If there is a poor match of interest, you shouldn't hire the person.

Test Results

Unless you live in a country that has laws to the contrary, I would not give out test results. Useful tests measure the subconscious traits of people, so if they see their results they will tend to disagree with them in an effort to prove the tests are invalid. Showing test results, no matter how accurate, can cause more problems than any good it might do. You could also give the candidate more ammunition to confuse you. If you are willing to counsel the successful applicants after they start working for you, then it is wise to show them the results. But never under any circumstances show them the attitude results.

What to Tell the Parting Applicant

If you're vague with applicants at the end of interviews, they can take that as a message that you're not interested in them, so they'll start looking elsewhere. The "We'll contact you" response, without explaining the process, is practically the same as saying you don't want them. Be clear about what happens next if you are interested in them.

Second Interviewer and Interviews

The interview process is an extremely important activity. In your early interviewing career, you may lack judgment on what is a good response and what isn't. You can overcome this by having an experienced person also interview the candidate and give you their opinion. If you are new to the hiring game, your best experience will come from comparing those you hired to the notes you took during your interviews. I highly recommend doing that.

Important hires, such as executives and people who will need a lot of time and money invested in them, should be interviewed by two or more people within the organization, as well as someone you respect and trust from outside the organization. My experience, as an outside interviewer, has saved many a company a lot of money by pointing out obvious faults they didn't originally see.

In most cases, interviewing an applicant several different times is more effective than trying to do it all at once. After the applicant leaves an interview, you may think of new questions to ask and areas to explore further. You can call the applicant if you think of further questions that you would like to ask. I've done complete interviews over the phone successfully for years, so don't think interviewing can only be done face-to-face. Although a face to face interview should be conducted before making a final decision.

Testing after the first interview is a good idea because it will show up traits that you can interview the next time the person comes in.

What's next?
There are many years of experience in these suggestions. You will make rapid improvements by re-reading this chapter and the next chapter several times, especially before interviews. You'll need experience *and* technique to become a good interviewer.

Chapter 10

Getting the Truth

A major challenge when interviewing an applicant is getting the truth. Most applicants stretch the truth or leave out vital facts to look better in an interview. Wolves and those who are truly incompetent know they need to cover that up, or they will never get the job. Therefore, the competent, good-natured people and the wolves or incompetents may sound very similar from surface answers.

Most applicants are poor judges of their own strengths and weaknesses. Some honestly believe they are better than they really are and try to persuade the interviewer to believe that, too. Therefore, it is up to the interviewer to figure out accurately and objectively, through all the misinformation and unreal assessments, just how good the person is.

Here are four basic interview approaches to get the truth:

* Second and third questioning.
* Promising to check references.
* Questioning the handling of situations.
* Verifying a questionable trait

Second and Third Questioning

Interviewing is not as easy as rolling right along asking prepared questions and whistling a merry tune, as the job seekers spill their guts. Even the best set of questions will not do that. Interviewing does require some alertness and judgment. Fortunately, a powerful technique that is especially effective for doing this is second and third questioning because it cuts below the superficial answers the candidate has thought up. It makes the difference between just having a conversation and really drilling down to the truth.

This technique asks questions about a person's answers; it is a follow-up type question. When the person answers your questions and leaves out some details, you ask her about it. If you still feel there are more details, you ask some more. Don't get me wrong; you're not giving a third degree. Ideally, you are projecting a strong interest in the area she brought up.

Also, when candidates say they have accomplished something great or did poorly on a job, there is still room for misunderstanding. Until you know the details, you may subconsciously add your own. For example, if a candidate said he helped the sales department produce two hundred percent of quota, you do not know how or why. If you think carefully, it could be any of the following reasons even if he was telling the truth.

* He could be a great salesperson.
* He could be an average salesperson.
* He could be a great leader.
* He could be a hard worker.
* The quota could have been low in the first place.
* He could have been an administrator.
* He could have been a good organizer.
* He could have assisted in the hiring of the people.

As you can see, the list could go on indefinitely. If you follow up with, "How did you help the department?" Now he says he administrated the department. Then another question reveals he did lots of errands and data input. By getting specifics, the true candidate appears.

Here is an example of second and third questioning about a surface comment, "I really did a good job by doing the accounting on that job":

First question: "What were your accomplishments on that job?"

Person says: "I also did all the bookkeeping."

Note: *At this point the interviewer is thinking, "Boy, we could use some backup accounting skill around here. I like this candidate, so won't waste my time thoroughly interviewing her."*

Second question: "What sort of bookkeeping did you do?"

Person says: "Everything the accountant didn't do."

Note: *At this point, the interviewer is thinking, "That makes sense. The applicant isn't an accountant."*

Third question: "What exactly did you do?"

Person says: "I wrote out checks and paid the bills. The Accountant did payroll, invoices, taxes, balanced the journals, etc."

Note: *The truth comes out. She only did a simple bookkeeping function.*

Here's another example to determine exactly how productive a candidate was at a previous job:

Interviewer: "What major achievements did you have on the XYZ production manager's job?"

Applicant: "I sold more products than some of the new salespeople, even though my main job was production manager."

Interviewer: "How did you do that?"

Applicant: "I took the sales calls if all the salespeople were out."

Interviewer: "How did you know how to close the sales?"

Applicant: "Well, I suppose I didn't. The people called in orders, so I didn't really have to sell them."

Asking for specific details causes the truth to come out. Applicants know once they start lying, they may end up contradicting themselves, and denied employment. It is also difficult for many people to lie to these types of direct questions.

Here is a List of Possible Second, Third and Fourth Questions:

* Why?
* What made you do that?
* What exactly did you do?
* What skills do you have that helped?
* How did you accomplish that?
* When did this happen and how long did it take?
* Who else contributed to that accomplishment? Anyone else?

Notice that these questions don't show your hand, so the answers will be valuable. One thing to watch in second and third questioning is not to indicate your doubts and concerns. You are just trying to find out more about a surface comment they made.

More good interview questions that get into more detail:

* When did that happen?
* What led up to that?
* What happened because of that?

* What did other employees say about it?
* How many times has that happened?
* What have you done to make sure it does not happen again?

Note-taking tool: A good way to get better at second and third questions is to take notes. Firstly, draw a line down the middle of your page. When you get surface comments, write them down on the left. Then, when you get down to specific useful information or traits, write them down on the right. The part in the right column would also contain direct observations of the candidate, such as "Compulsive talker, won't listen." Look at the notes in both columns to judge the candidate.

Sample:

Enjoyed my job.	Especially loved teaching people.
My boss let me stay around for a long time after the project was finished.	Wanted to get really good at ABC programming.
I was a good systems engineer.	Serious, not animated

Promising to Check References

If people are convinced you will check their references, they will be more honest with you. The process of convincing starts after the rapport-building conversation at the beginning of an interview. Inform applicants of the following:

* It is important we have a good match.
* In addition to these interviews, I intend to check with past bosses and supervisors.
* You will have the opportunity to interview our staff. (This will give them the feeling that you are interested in a good match, and you are trying to be fair.)

What the applicants think their previous bosses will say about them is important information to get. The best question to ask regarding this is "What is your best guess of what your boss really felt at that time were your strengths, weaker points, and overall performance?" If the person can't think of any weaker points, you should use a pregnant pause or repeat the question with an emphasis on the word *guess*. If he can't even guess, you should ask for his self-appraisal at that time. Do not go any further back than ten years for midlevel people. You can stretch that to fifteen years if she only had a few supervisors, but never go beyond twenty years unless the person has a clear recall of that time.

Asking candidates what they think their supervisors would say about specific performance accomplishments can help check for exaggeration. Most candidates will backpedal if they over stated an accomplishment facing the fact you may validate their claim.

Asking applicants for permission to call the reference when the name first comes up further convinces applicants you will check. In addition to getting permission during the interview, you can request the supervisor's phone number, which will further convince the applicant of your intention to call. When you ask for references at the end of the interview, the effect of keeping them honest will be lost.

Questioning the Handling of Situations

A good way to check competency is to ask applicants how they handled situations. Ask them for the biggest problems they had at previous jobs. When they offer a situation, ask how they handled it. After they tell you what they did, ask them why they did it that way. For example, ask salespeople for the most common objections they encountered while selling a product and how they dealt with those objections.

Another way is to ask for a demonstration. For instance, have them sell you the product they used to sell, and see how they do. Do not ask them to sell your product or an item on your desk, as that will only test ability to think on one's feet. If the person is applying for an administrative assistant position, put them on the computer and ask them to do things. All you have to do is ask yourself, "Would the person be competent enough to handle the types of problems that occur in my company?" Please make allowances for the fact that the person is in a strange environment and being watched

As I mentioned previously, the candidates are not objective about their strengths and weaknesses. You on the other hand, have the advantage of comparing one candidate against another and to past and existing employees. Based on these comparisons, you should have a good idea about competence.

Verifying a Questionable Trait

Sometimes you will know of a candidate's bad trait but not know how bad it really is. This could occur after testing, interviewing, or reference checking. If you have a good testing program, this should not happen, as good tests have bar charts or lines to demonstrate it. If you have not tested the candidate, and the candidate or reference says something to indicate a weak trait, you may end up with a question mark.

Our first impulse is to just ask the candidate how bad the trait is and hope to get an truthful answer. First, even if he were trying to be honest, he wouldn't really know, or would down play it. Second, he can figure out your concern and work to convince you that your concern is unfounded.

The good news about verifying traits is the time to prepare for it. The concerns usually come after the candidate has left the first interview and you have gone through your notes. The difficulty comes in knowing what to ask without giving away the profile or concern. Preparing for the follow up interview is the most important part of the interview process.

I will cover the types of approaches that you can successfully take.

What ifs: A *what if* question is a made up scenario that requires the candidate to say what they would do in a circumstance. These questions are only successful if the examples have been well prepared and do not give away your concerns. Effective *what if* questions show how the candidate handles difficult situations. For example, ask candidates what they would do if their boss specifically asks them to lie on a delivery date that is twice as soon as reality, and to explain their answer. If they respond that they would have a hard time with that, don't be surprised; you put them in a difficult situation and they are avoiding your question. Under these circumstances, it is important that you then repeat the question, for example, "Okay, but what would you do and why?" This will give you clues about honesty and support. *What if* questions have been prepared for some of the attitude traits and found in the interview questions chapter, which comes next.

Likes and likes the least: Any dislike will usually turn out to be a weakness or avoidance after the honeymoon period is over. Candidates don't usually mind telling you what they like the least, especially if you ask them for their likes as well. So if you have a concern about something, you can ask for what they like the most and like the least about the activity surrounding your concern. For example, in sales you suspect the candidate may not be assertive enough to close sales. In this case, ask her what she likes the most and least about closing sales. Do not ask, "Are you assertive when it comes to closing?" because that would give away your concern, and even the most unassertive closer will assert how assertive they are at closing sales. The *likes* and *dislike* questions are useful because they don't give away your concern and the answers actually mean something. If that doesn't get your confirmation on assertiveness, you could ask what are their likes and dislikes about selling in general, presentations, meeting with several prospects at the same time and so on.

The one drawback with this type of questioning is not insisting the candidate give you a dislike answer. This formula for detecting the extent of a concern is figuring out which activity would involve the concern and without asking about the concern directly, ask the candidate about *likes* and *likes the least* about that activity. This is especially useful if you can get the candidate to tell you about an experience he had with this and what he did about it.

Effective and least effective: Asking candidates about areas in which they are most effective and least effective is similar to *likes and likes the least*. The simple way to explain this approach is to use the *like's* section above; replace *likes* and *least likes* with *effective* and *least effective*. Whether you use *likes* or *effective* type questions depends on the concern and gives you a chance to vary your questioning. For example, you want to know if a manager candidate is afraid of taking risks. You could use the *effective* or *least effective* question about the subject of making decisions. If you asked *likes* and *dislikes* you may not find out what you want. In this example, you would be even more effective getting the candidate to tell you about an actual experience.

Philosophy questions: Asking candidates about their philosophy on a certain subject is similar to the *likes* and *effective* questions. Let's say you are concerned that your candidate may not get back to customers with bad news on a timely basis. You determine the activity is customer service. The next step is to ask for their philosophy about customer service. When the candidate makes a statement like, "You need to keep the customer happy," you could then ask but how do you do that? If the answer is "never say anything to upset the customer," you have more confirmation this candidate may be too nice for what you want. You could ask a second question requesting that the candidate explain their philosophy about that.

Remember, not to ask a semi-specific question giving away your concern, such as how would you keep a customer happy if you had bad news to tell them. This would give away your concern and they would most likely explain how they would tell the bad news immediately.

You could also vary the philosophy wording to beliefs, thoughts, or have the candidate give you a mini lecture on the activity as if she is teaching you. Similar to the likes and effective questions, you are going to be much more effective if the candidates can tell you about actual experiences and how they handled them.

Greatest achievements and greatest failures: This technique asks for actual experiences with follow up second and third questions. With the applicant's questionable trait in mind, decide what the action related to the concern is. Then ask about his greatest achievement with that activity, as well as how he could have been more successful (a nice and more effective way of asking for failures). The problem with this question occurs when the candidate cannot think of anything. In this case, inform the candidate you have plenty of time and let them think about it some more.

In the beginning, you may feel frustrated and impatient that you can't ask candidates directly about their faults, but as your experience grows you will find this skill is easy to learn.

By employing these approaches, you can determine your concerns about a candidate by going through the above questions and writing out the most effective questions to ask. As you ask these questions, also note the degree of negativity that may come up. For example, a "Hate to do that" is more negative than, "I prefer not to deal with that."

Utilize this procedure with every candidate until it becomes second nature. With good second and third questions, you will be able to predict accurately how new employees will turn out in reality.

To Win or Not to Win?

Getting to the truth of a candidate's presentation is always a challenge. It is like a game where the candidate tries to look better while you try to understand reality, and at the same time act nicely without showing your hand. I hope that you can study these ideas enough to give you an ongoing success.

To make things simpler, follow the procedure outlined in the next chapter on interview questions. Many of the concerns mentioned have already been answered.

Chapter 11

Interview Questions

These sets of questions will not make up for poor interviewing skills. However, they will help you detect good applicants no matter how good you are, as long as you follow the instructions that go with each question.

If you have read the previous chapters, you will know that the first answer a person gives to your question is somewhat superficial. You will need to "drill down" on the candidate's answers to find out the most useful information. You will notice that follow up questions accompany most of these questions. There are some additional follow up questions at the end of the chapter you can use with just about any initial question.

This chapter is made up of two sets of questions designed for two or more interviewing days. These questions will cover most of the important subjects affecting a good hiring decision. These subjects amount to twelve different queries as follows:

1. Does the candidate have all the skills to do the work?
2. Does the candidate have the education to do the work?
3. Does the candidate have the experience to do the work?
4. Is the candidate bright enough, quick enough, creative enough?

5. Will the candidate be satisfied with the amount of money and benefits the company can afford to pay?
6. Does the candidate have a good nature (Hard worker, positive, responsible, truthful, loyal, and supportive? Not a wolf or criminal?).
7. Will the candidate fit into the culture of the company?
8. Does the candidate have the right personality for the work?
9. Does the candidate have the interest in doing the work?
10. Does the candidate like working inside (desk jockey) or outside?
11. Will the candidate be able to meet the company's attendance requirements?
12. Does the candidate have the ability to perform specific job functions, with or without special accommodation? (See Americans with Disabilities Act in the chapter on legal questioning).

Should there be a Second Day's Interview or Not?

You are unlikely to cover all these areas with an applicant in a one-hour interview. Therefore, you either extend the interview or have the candidate come back. What you do on the second day depends on some of the following:

* Is this person applying for a minimum wage job, an important midlevel position or an executive type position, such as a Vice President?
* Do you use assessments to help cover some of the areas?
* Does the company's hiring process require others to interview?
* Do you prefer doing reference checking before or in the middle of interviewing?
* How much phone interviewing was done before the first interview?

Let's examine each of these items in further detail.

Is This Person Applying for a Minimum Wage Job or an Executive Position?

Interviewing a person for a minimum wage job could be effectively done in an hour, plus a few competency tests. On the other hand, if you were hiring a Vice President, you may do four 2 hour interviews, give personality testing, perform extensive reference checking and ask all your Vice Presidents to interview the applicant as well. None of the following sets of questions would fit perfectly for these two different types of candidates. For the minimum wage person, you may ask some question from each set of questions. For the Vice President, you would need all two separate sets plus a chronological interview. These sets of questions are tailored for jobs just above minimum wage and below top executive levels.

Do You Use Assessments to Help Cover Some of the Areas?

Testing makes a big difference in how much interviewing you will need to do. If you test for skills, attitude, and personality, you can reduce the need to interview mid-level applicants by several hours per person. This is because you will only need to focus on what showed up on the results as possible concerns. The tests could eliminate any need for more interviewing if the results clearly show the person will not fit the company or position. (Warning: Using any tests as a sole method of screening can be illegal.)

Testing after the first major phone or in-person interview usually saves the most time and energy.

Does the Company's Hiring Process Require Others to Interview?

If others will be interviewing the candidate, they can use these sets of questions. It will not be a good idea for each person to be asking the same questions, so the questions and subjects can be divided up by areas of expertise. For example, one can check skills, education and experience; another can check attitude and cultural fit; another can check personality fit; another can do the rest. Some repeat questions are OK to check for consistency or to dig deeper into a subject you are unsure about.

Do You Prefer Doing Reference Checking Before or in the Middle of Interviewing?

Well done reference checking after the first interview should not reduce the need to use the sets of questions. This is because reference checking primarily helps to validate what a candidate says and secondly to find out more about the candidate.

How Much Phone Interviewing was Done Before the First Interview?

If you asked all the first day's set of interview questions over the phone, then you would go to the second day's set of questions on the first day's in-person interview. If you asked less than all the questions, then you would complete the first day's interview questions before you start on the second day's questions. Questions asked over the phone are almost the same as if they were asked in person.

Pre-interviewing Formalities

* Make copies of the set of questions you will need. I give you permission to make copies of the questions, for interviewing.
* You may need to fill in answers for question #8 and #13 on the first day's set of questions (See Chapter Seven).
* Set up a place away from other people where you can interview someone.
* Study the candidate's resume and get prepared mentally for what you intend to ask.
* Create a friendly atmosphere for candidates by introducing yourself and offering refreshments. Get into some small talk but keep it to a minimum.
* Explain that you will do thorough reference checks if the interview goes well. (The purpose of this is to keep the candidate thinking you will check the validity of her answers.)

Put it in Writing
It is highly advisable to write down your answers for the following reasons:

* So that you can go back over your notes before making decisions about the candidate.
* So that you have something to go back and review after the person has been working for about a year to help improve your interviewing skills.
* That if you are accused of asking illegal questions, you will have notes to help prove otherwise.
* It may help you listen better.

Have your set of questions already copied so all you have to do is fill in the blanks. You don't need to be burdened in the middle of an interview rewriting the questions you are asking. Also, what you write down will be easier to understand later knowing what the question was.

First Day's Set of Questions
The purpose of the first day's set of questions is to make sure the candidate is qualified enough to interview in more depth.

Use this set of questions to ask and listen, rather than wasting your time explaining, selling or talking. Only at the end should you ask them for questions they may have. You do this mainly to see what their attention is focused on, not to lecture or sell them. An interviewer should not talk more than 30% of the time during the entire interview. Interviewing is the act of asking questions, not explaining. I have found the activity of just asking questions sells the organization better than anything else because they can tell you and your company are professional.

The information given below explains more about the questions used on the *first day's set of questions*. About one paragraph has been devoted to each question.

You should start by asking questions about their interest in the job in order to bridge into the interview and to understand their interest in the job.

Then ask about their skills, education, and experience to determine how competent they may be. For example, let us say you are looking of an administrative assistant and a *must have* for that position is word processing experience. On his resume he lists "computer knowledge" as a skill. You ask the person about their knowledge of computers and the person says, "How to send and receive emails, but nothing about word processing." Now the candidate has admitted they are not qualified and you don't need to waste any more time.

Following that, you should ask the candidate about her resume if it didn't clearly show a job history. The purpose should be to find out about gaps between employment and frequency of job changes. Big gaps and frequent changes are indicators of attitude issues.

Next, you are wise to find out how successful the person was in previous positions by asking the candidate about successes stated in the resume. By writing this down, you can check it against later information you discover. For example, the candidate tells you she sold 4 million dollars of real estate in 1998 at an average of 2 percent commission after deducting expenses. You later see a copy of a tax report (W2) that indicates she only made half of what she said.

After checking successes, ask for more information about the candidate's main activities using the resume as a guide. Look for similar or dissimilar personality type activities the applicant did. Find out what he liked doing the most and what he liked doing the least. (Personality verification.)

The next question is a little unusual and takes a little thought before the interview starts. It involves asking about common concerns involving a position. For example, in a sales position many of the previous candidates had resistance to learning about the product and failed. Finding out about willingness to learn products, in this example, would be important. This subject of common concerns is covered in detail in Chapter Seven.

At this point, the interview changes again. It consists of a package several questions asked repeatedly. It commences with a question of who the candidate's supervisor was, which subtly communicates that information is likely to be checked. Next, rather than asking for strengths and weaknesses, ask for the applicant's guess of what the supervisor may have thought about the candidate.

The next question in the package asks for the reasons why people left their past jobs. As you know, most people are ready with good answers for leaving a job. I suggest asking questions about their reasons until their story truly makes sense. You need to drill down on these answers to find out really why they left. For example, if the person said he left because of a school conflict, then ask a question about what changed the priority?

Your main reason for asking why a person left a previous position should be to detect disloyal type answers. For example, if you hear the reason for leaving was for a little more money or other minor benefit, you can put that down as a disloyal type indicator. In our culture, at this time, leaving for a little more money is so accepted you may not realize there is anything wrong with it. But there is. Leaving for a lot more money makes more sense and may not be an attitude indicator. Asking questions in this way will help you assess the candidate's loyalty, agenda, character traits, and most importantly—attitude.

The next step involves the candidate's interest in the kind of work you are offering. Find out what the candidate is looking for in his next job.

Now if you have time, ask about those skills, that education and that experience the candidate didn't bring up in question 2 that you know should be there. One way of checking for these in an interview is to ask about nomenclature and procedures that only a skilled person would know.

If you still have time, ask for what they liked most or least about positions they talk about. The first answers will be socially acceptable ones. Therefore, ask about these answers and do not accept general ones, such as nothing, everything, or nothing else. These deeper answers will help tell you if they have the right personality for the position.

Finally, learn more about a candidate by her questions. For example, a question like, "Will I have an administrative assistant?" tells you that lack of one could be an issue after the honeymoon period is over. If your answer is "No, you won't have an administrative assistant" and she says, "That's Okay," you should probe further, because it is more likely she doesn't like your decision, despite what she said.

FIRST DAY'S SET OF QUESTIONS
(Prepare for questions 8 & 17 before interview.)

CANDIDATE'S NAME: _____

DATE: _____

1. Why are you interested in applying for this job?
2. What skills, education and experience do you have for this job?
3. What major accomplishments did you achieve with each one of those skills or experiences? (If necessary, ask questions to get specifics.)
4. Question job history and gaps if they are unclear on the resume
5. Question statements of success in a resume. How did you accomplish that result? Get details and examples. Find out who else was involved.
6. What main activities have you done for a living?
7. What other main activities have you done for a living?
8. (List problems usually associated with the position you are trying to fill. See Chapter Seven.)
9. Ask questions to see if candidate will be able to overcome these common stumbling blocks.
10. Who was your supervisor on your last job?
11. What do you think he/she felt at that time were your:
    a) strengths?
    b) weaknesses?
12. Why did you leave that job (or are intending to leave that job)?
13. (Keep questioning his/her answers until it makes more sense.)
14. Repeat this line of questioning for at least three of the candidate's last supervisors. For higher-level positions you will want to go back at least 5 supervisors.
15. What are you looking for in your next position?
16. (Keep questioning these answers to make more sense)
17. (Before the first interview list all the must have skills, experience, and education for the position.)

18. (Ask questions about these skills [not discussed by the candidate on questions 2 &3] to determine if they understand the nomenclature and the correct procedures for the activity. For example, don't assume that just because they say they can word process means they can do it to the degree you would like.)
19. What do/did you like the most about your last position?
20. What do/did you dislike most about your last position? (First answers are usually only politically correct.)
21. What about that didn't you like?
22. Do you have any questions for me? (Note the questions asked, as they will tell you what is important to this applicant. Write them all down and think about them later.)

Mini Historical or Chronological Interview
(rather than asking questions 1 to 22 above)
If you are reasonably sure the candidate is likely to fit the desired profile, then the following can be a more effective way to conduct the first interview, even though it will take longer. This depends a lot on the interviewer.

If you are interviewing a person for a senior executive position, you should do this as well as all the other questions in this chapter.

Have candidates tell you about their work experiences from the earliest jobs in high school forward. As the applicant talks, ask some of the "First day's Set of Questions" as they apply to each job they tell you about, for example, *so why did you leave that job or what did you like most and least about that job?* Because this will most likely be the first interview with limited time, make sure you cover all the positions with the most time spent on the current or last position. By getting a general overview of each position, you will learn what concerns need to be covered in future interviews. In this way, you will get an excellent sense of what your candidates are likely to do in the future.

What to Tell the Candidate before He Leaves.
Clearly explain the next step to the candidate. If you feel the candidate might be a good fit, you should indicate your interest. Otherwise, the candidate is likely to put out more resumes and accept another job. If you are not interested in this candidate or not sure, try the following: "At this time I have other people coming in. I'll let you know if I need to ask you any more questions."

Inform the applicant of the next step (It is vital to make this clear). Set up the next appointment if all goes well or set the expectation for a return call. If you do this you can make it clear to an applicant if a certain period of time has passed you are no longer interested.

If all has gone well, this is the best time to have the candidate do assessments and tests.

Designing the Interviews

Each company should design interviews for their own requirements. This should include how long the interviews will be, how many interviews, any new tests, and number of interviewers. For example, some companies looking for commissioned salespeople may want to place more emphasis on *selling* the applicant on the job.

Second Day's Set of Questions

Before you can make the candidate an offer, you should ideally know that all your concerns have been answered. So on the second day, you should have two objectives. The first is to answer any concerns you may have about the candidate. The second objective is the check into areas that you haven't examined yet.

List all the concerns about the candidate as you go over your notes and memory of the first interview. The list of areas not covered yet should be determined by going over the 12 different queries (mentioned above).

The second day's set of questions are laid out under these 12 different queries. Don't waste your time asking a candidate all these questions. Instead, before the candidate arrives, look over your list of concerns and areas you haven't interviewed yet and mark the questions you still need to ask. On the first 3 queries—skills, education and experience—you may need to write down which specific ones you are still not sure about.

To save valuable time and energy you might first address the major concerns that don't look good. Note these questions as top priority. For example, because of some contradictions from the first day's interview, you should note the honesty questions as a high priority under query 6 "Does the candidate have a good nature." Next, you would go through the 12 query headings noting what questions to ask.

When the candidate comes in for the second day interviews, you can ask the questions in the priority you have worked out. If at any time you discover the candidate is clearly unsuitable, you should end the interview. On the other hand, if nothing obviously negative comes up, you should continue until all your questions have been answered.

Before you begin interviewing, look at query 7, on culture at page 11-21. Culture, by the way, is the unwritten behavior of an organization. You should mark what your company's answers would be to the culture questions so that you can more objectively compare them to a candidate's answers. You will only need to do this once for all future interviewing. So the more accurately you can answer the questions the better. You may want to consider an outside person to help with a more objective result. You may also want to consider the culture of the department the person will be working in, as each department may have a different culture.

You should also establish the ideal personality for the position before interviewing for it. This is covered under query 8 "Does the candidate have the right personality for the work?" If you are not familiar with the four main personality types, then you will have to skip this step. Even if you don't know about personality types, you can always ask questions that detect if the candidate enjoyed doing a similar type of work.

Second Day's Set of Questions

1. **Does the Candidate Have all the Skills to do the Work?**

   List the skills you are not sure the candidate has.

   a. SKILL: What level of competency do you have with (name the skill)?

   Ask questions about the answer to determine specifically what they have been able to do. Does the person know the nomenclature?

   Do this for each skill that is critical for success in this position.

2. **Does the Candidate Have the Education to do the Work?**

   List the types and levels of education you are not sure the candidate has.

   a. EDUCATION LEVEL: What was the highest level of education you achieved at (name the type of institution, i.e., college)?

   b. What subjects did you study or major in?

   Ask questions about the answer to determine specifically what they studied and what level of competency the person achieved. This is important to help verify this person actually achieved the education level they stated on their resume.

   If the candidate does not have the education credentials, he or she has gained the education in other ways.

   c. Tell me about any education you have received outside a regular school program.

3. **Does the Candidate Have the Experience to do the Work?**

    List the types of experience you are not sure the candidate has.

    a. EXPERIENCE: What length of experience do you have with (name the experience)?

    Ask questions about the answer to determine specifically what the person did.

4. **Is the candidate bright enough, quick enough, creative enough?**

    General observation of the candidate, sample presentations, examining work she or he has done, and timed tests are the only good ways to check brightness, quickness and creativeness. General observation during an interview will not by itself detect brightness, quickness and creativeness.

5. **Will the candidate be satisfied with the amount of money and benefits the company can afford to pay?**

    These questions should be the last ones to ask candidates before making them an offer.

    a. How much were you paid on your last position?

    b. Did you get any other benefits?

    c. How many hours per week did you have to work to get that?

    d. What are you hoping to be paid for this position?

    e. Why do you feel justified in asking for that?

6. Does the Candidate Have a Good Nature (Attitude)?

Questioning a person in depth on why he left each job is one way to detect attitude problems. If you have already done that and still have questions about the candidate's attitude, you should skip the questions about leaving jobs. If the candidate was fired, first to be laid off, upset with management, left for minor selfish reasons, or had too many disagreements, then these symptoms indicate attitude problems.

a. Why did you leave your last position? [*if you are not sure*]

Keep questioning these answers to make more sense.

Keep questioning these answers to make sense. It's a bit repetitive but critical for trying to get the most truthful answer.

b. Go through at least three of the candidate's last positions. For more senior positions go through at least 5 positions.

Good general attitude questions:

c. What are your goals in life?

Good attitude people will usually be more interested in making a difference in the world; poor attitude people will usually be more interested in making money.

d. What was an example from your past where a boss demanded something or some way of doing something that you didn't agree with? [*Ask for more details.*] If I were talking to that boss, what would her/his opinion have been?

Observe how cooperative the candidate is.

IT IS VERY IMPORTANT TO ASK THIS SECOND SET OF QUESTIONS.

e. What was another example of a boss demanding something or some way of doing something that you didn't agree with? [*Ask for more details.*] If I were talking to that boss, what would his/her opinion have been?

• • •

Concern: DISHONESTY

f. Try this situational question first: "Let's say the boss asked you to lie to a customer by saying the product would be delivered in two weeks. You know it will take four weeks, and the boss knows it too. What would you do?"

Make sure the candidate actually *answers the question, "What would you do?"*

If he says he would lie, you know you have a person who will lie. If he says he would never lie under any circumstance, then that is a good indicator. Anything in between is a gray area. The best response would be the candidate hesitating a lot and saying that it is a hard choice, but she wouldn't lie. Ideally, the candidate would want to discuss the matter with the boss and work out a different plan of action to achieve the same result—without lying. Ignore all the sales talk they may give, such as, "I would feel uncomfortable lying and don't believe lying is right." Instead, repeat the question, "But what would you do?"

g. Try this situational question also: "Let's say the customer agrees to give you the contract if you can deliver in two weeks. What would you do if you knew you couldn't deliver for four weeks?"

Reference checks will not determine honesty. Only by testing and asking the candidate good questions can you determine honesty.

h. Here is another *what-if* situation: "The boss leaves a confidential, private memo on his desk and one of his employees reads it. Who is mostly to blame?"

    If the answer is both, that is a red flag in regards to honesty. Employees should not be reading private memos on the boss's desk.

i. What do you base your opinion on?

    Tip: Honesty can only be determined if you put applicants in difficult positions, and then see which route they take.

• • •

Concern: LAZY

The best way to detect laziness is to give applicants difficult hypothetical situations, and then ask them what they would do.

j. Here is a *what-if* question: "You have been at work 8 hours for a company that doesn't have a late shift, but the customer's job you have been working on needs to be completed that night. Your boss insists it is perfectly Okay if you go home now. The only commitment you have for that night is going to dinner with your spouse. What would you do, and what would you think about your decision?"

    If the person says, "It depends," that's already a negative. Find out what they are thinking, because therein lies their value system.

k. What do you think of work environments that require 45- to 50-hour work-weeks to meet customer demands?

Question the applicant's answer.

l. Do you prefer the *thinking* side of a job or the *doing* side of a job? Why is that your preference?

Tip: Don't communicate the profile or the answers you would like to hear. Instead, ask questions for which the correct answer is difficult to determine. For example, don't ask, "What would you do if you had to work a 12-hour day to get a project out?" (The obvious answer you're looking for is that you would work 12 hours a day until the project is complete, whereas the previous questions give no clue of what you are looking for.)

• • •

Concern: TOO CRITICAL

m. Name of the last supervisor you worked for?

n. What did you admire most about that supervisor?

o. What didn't you admire about that supervisor?

p. What ideas did you agree about with this supervisor?

q. What ideas didn't you agree about with this supervisor?

Repeat this line of questioning for at least 3 of the candidates last supervisors. For senior-level positions go through at least 5 supervisors.

If the candidate is highly critical of more than one out of four supervisors, the candidate is likely to have a critical attitude problem.

TIP: Don't ask, "Are you too critical?" as that question gives applicants the clue to say "no!" no matter what they truly believe.

• • •

Concern: LACK OF SUPPORT

r. What do you think your boss should do for you?

s. Here is another *what-if* situation: "If a coworker came to you with a project he wanted done, but your boss also came to you with a project he wanted done—both needed to be done immediately and both were equally important—how would you deal with that? Why would you deal with it that way?"

Any answer that indicates it is the boss's job to help them get the job done is reverse delegation and a red flag. The boss may be expected to train, lead, and inform but not do what the employee was hired to get done.

Also, see important attitude questions already covered by 5b at the beginning of this section.

• • •

Concern: BLAME

t. What are your thoughts about a boss who requires you to commit to a quarterly quota?

u. What do you feel a fair boss should think if you are unable to make those numbers because your resources are breaking down?

If you get a "It depends" answer, then give these examples: "The machine you use for your job broke down; the main vendor you use got behind; your assistant kept taking days off." Now ask the question again.

If the candidates think the boss should be lenient, that is an indication of blame. If they say they should make the numbers despite the problems, ask them this:

v. Why would that be fair?

If they haven't already given their opinions, ask for them:

w. Why do you feel your answers are the best way to think about this subject?

The more they believe it is their responsibility to make the numbers the better. The response, "I would go to my boss and tell him or her that the quarterly numbers might not happen" doesn't tell you much by itself. Make sure he answered the questions.

x. What do you feel a fair boss should think about you if your commute causes you to be 10 minutes late twice a week?

If they think their boss should understand, this is an indication of blame. If they say their boss should not accept that behavior, ask them this:

y. Why would a fair boss not accept that?

If they haven't already given their opinion, ask this:

z. What is your opinion about this subject?

TIP: If you ask a question like, "Are you responsible?" or, "Do you blame?" you are projecting what you want and will get good answers, even from people with major blame traits.

7. **Will the Candidate Fit into the Culture of the Company?**

   If your company has high standards of honesty, integrity, responsibility, work ethic, and a good balance of appreciation and criticalness, then you can mostly depend on a person with a good attitude to fit in.

   The following can be given to the candidate to circle the applicable answers. Or the interviewer can ask the questions and circle the answers.

   a. Tell me a company in the last ten years that you felt good working for. Which department?

   If he can't think of a company he worked for, get one he/she admired.

   b. Did the management of that department permit some
      * exaggeration
      * minor exaggeration
      * no exaggeration?

c. What size was the company you worked for?
   * over 300 people
   * 40 to 299 people
   * fewer than 40 people

d. Was the company run as if it was:
   * new
   * established
   * leadership wanting to retire
   * trying to improve
   * trying for some improvement
   * trying to remain the same
   * businesslike
   * businesslike but laid back
   * laid back
   * risk taking
   * taking some risk
   * careful
   * expecting long hours
   * expecting little extra hours
   * expecting regular hours

e. How important was keeping customers satisfied by that management?
   * important
   * mostly important
   * sometimes important

f. Which of those did you disagree with at the time and how would you have preferred it?

g. Why did you disagree with those ones?

8. **Does the Candidate Have the Right Personality for the Work?**

   a. What work activities do you like doing the most?

   b. What about those activities do you like doing the most? Why?

   c. What work activities do you dislike doing the most?

   Don't accept there are none.

   d. What about those activities do you dislike the most? Why?

   e. What other work activities do you like doing the most?

   Keep digging. A candidate's initial answers are probably superficial. Challenging them to think harder about these questions will reveal more truths about the individual.

   f. What about those activities do you like doing the most? Why?

   g. What other work activities do you dislike doing the most?

   Don't accept there are none.

   h. What about those activities do you dislike the most? Why?

   i. From all the jobs you've had, which part of which job were you the most effective at and which parts were you the least effective at? Why do you think that is?

   j. What subjects at school did you do well in and what subjects did you do poorly in?

9. **Does the Candidate Have the Interest in Doing the Work?**

    a. What other positions would you consider?

    b. What would be the ideal position for you? Why do feel that is the ideal position for you?

    c. What changes in the position you are interviewing for could make it a more ideal for you? Why do you feel that would make it more ideal for you?

    d. If things went well for you, what position would you like to end up in? Why do you feel that would be an ideal position for you in the future?

    e. What positions in the past didn't work well for you?

    f. What positions in the past did work well for you? Why do you think those positions worked well for you?

    g. What were your early interests and ambitions, even if they sound silly now? What made them seem interesting?

    h. What personal interests do you have?

    Don't question or write down private matters such as family and religion. Stick with hobbies and extracurricular activities.

10. **Does the Candidate Like Working Inside (Desk Jockey) or Outside?**

    a. In the past, have you preferred jobs that are done inside at a desk or on the outside?

b. In the future, will you prefer a job that is done inside, outside or in between?

11. **Will the candidate be able to meet the company's attendance requirements?**

    a. What days of the week will you be available to work?

    b. What hours will you be available to work during those days?

12. **Does the candidate have the ability to perform specific job junctions, with or without special accommodation?**

    The Americans with Disabilities Act prohibits any pre-employment questions about disabilities. To avoid legal problems, focus on the candidate's ability to perform the job—not on the disability. (See Chapter Thirteen, your Human Resource Manager or a good labor attorney if you have questions and concerns.)

    a. Are you able to perform this work with or without some sort of modification of our facility or our job description?

    If the candidate indicates she/he does need some sort of modification, ask the following:

    b. What sort of modification would you need and how would you perform the job with these changes?

General follow up questions:

a. How did you feel about that?

b. Why did you do what you did?

c. What thoughts did you have?

d. How did you approach that situation?

e. Why did you do what you did?

f. How could you have done that differently?

g. Would you change your approach in hind sight?

h. Do you regret you decision?

i. What did you learn from that experience?

j. Why is that important to you?

k. Why did that go so well?

l. Describe a situation related to this topic.

m. Give me some examples of a related situation.

Leading questions: (How to make a candidate feel at ease and open up)

a. We have all been in that position at some point. When have you?

b. I remember a time this happened to me. How about you?

c. It is natural for people to have feelings about this topic. When have you had feelings about a similar situation?

See chapter 16 for some more specific personality, behavioral, competency and Attitude questions. These can be used throughout the interview to uncover more specific areas of importance.

I give my permission to copy these forms for interviewing, not for republication.

Chapter 12

Reference Checks

Checking references is a necessary and worthwhile activity. You check references to verify resumes and to find out strengths and weaknesses that didn't surface during interviewing. It will also help sort out any remaining puzzles or concerns about an applicant.

The idea of calling complete strangers and asking them about someone you barely know can sound intimidating. In reality, references consider it part of their job to accept calls about their past employees, even in cases they really don't want to say anything. What I think is contrary to most peoples beliefs is the fact most of them will return your call as if you were a new customer. From my experience, the more conversations you have checking references, the easier it gets.

The Challenges

The concern with reference checks is that former employers know they can get into legal problems caused by saying the wrong thing. Employers are afraid of former employees suing them for libel, defamation of character, or invasion of privacy. Their fear is justified because one small unintentional mistake can cost millions of dollars to settle.

These legal problems occur when the previous manager gives false information or opinions that cause another employer to turn down the applicant. The following are a few (not all) ways a former employer can get into legal problems:

* Saying a person was guilty of a crime when a court hadn't reached a conviction or the person hadn't admitted guilt.
* Giving out informal information on a former employee, especially of a negative nature. For example, saying the employee was lazy, untrustworthy, and sometimes unreliable.
* Giving out information from subjective employee reviews without backup documentation. For example, "We rated his attitude below average."

Therefore, some companies train their managers on what to say or not to say in reference checks. It is usually brilliantly simple—don't say anything.

If you don't do reference checks, you increase the chance of being sued for negligent hiring. Negligent hiring is the legal name for hiring someone without sufficient pre-employment checking who hurts a coworker. For instance, the person has a criminal record as a sex offender or theft and commits one of these crimes on a company employee.

There is an answer.

Some Employers Will Give References

Despite all the negatives and a survey showing that nearly half of all companies have a policy against giving out references, supervisors are willing to give out dates of employment, positions held and to verify salary. But, in reality, a high percentage of former managers will help you way more than that.

Most applicants have already talked their past supervisors into giving good references. If you have any problem, I have found the candidates will call them for you and make it Okay. This is an important point, if the candidates had a good rapport with their past supervisors the candidate will be able to find a way for you to speak candidly with that supervisor.

When you add more or different references than the applicant had originally intended to give you, your percentage of who will talk to you might drop off. This happens when marginal or weak employees give you names during an interview that they hoped you wouldn't ask about. Starting out, you may not want to tackle these types until your confidence improves.

What I have found is that former employers are willing to return my calls and to talk to me in direct proportion to the quality of the applicant. Fortunately, I have never known a client to get into legal problems for giving out employee information.

Additionally, as you and I know, it is wise to deal ethically with any information gained from a reference. If you do decide to turn a candidate down for a poor reference don't tell them who said what and why specifically. Stick to a broad statement, "your references identified some areas of concern that cause us to believe you may not a be a great match for this position." And leave it at that repeat that line as many times as needed, but never elaborate.

How to Open Up a Reference

If a manager tells you he can't talk about a former employee, the first action you should attempt to do is establish better rapport. For example, discuss the general problem of getting accurate information about applicants. Once you've established good rapport, your job will become much easier. When you tell the reference that what they say will be kept confidential, it does help. If it is true, you can state that it is your company's policy not to hire anyone without this reference information. As a last resort, you can call back again at a later time and talk to the manager's boss.

Some people say you must convince the former manager or employer that the information you are requesting is vital. It must have been a good writer with no experience. In reality, that is not true or doesn't seem to make any difference. Most of these supervisors are savvy about the legal consequences but will talk to you in a guarded way. It is almost as if they keep telling themselves, "Be careful not to really tell the truth about this person. I owe it to this poor sap to give 'em a clue or two." So once you get them going, they seem to get a bit of confidence and give you clues, even though they know they shouldn't. You on the other hand, need to be just as savvy of the clues they give you. Even when supervisors are unwilling to give references, you still learn something—the applicant has at least one annoying trait.

Whom should I Call?

You should start with the applicant's former supervisors or managers he's had in the last five to ten years. If you have been interviewing well, you will have names and numbers of supervisors to call. The most current references are the most important. Unfortunately, the best person to call is the supervisor the applicant had problems with and the one he doesn't want you to call. After you've called the person's previous supervisors, you can also call the supervisors' managers.

Calling subordinates, major customers, or anyone else who would be aware of the applicant's work habits is almost a waste of time. These references can be very deceiving. I remember a candidate who could only give me her previous subordinates. They all had wonderful things to say because she apparently always agreed with their disagreements with management. This led me to discover that she, in a supervisor role, was not supportive of her boss. I was lucky to find that nugget. When you talk to these people, you will seldom find out anything. In fact, the glowing descriptions can mislead the best of us.

Personnel or human resource people are only good for employment dates, salary ranges, and job titles. This is useful as it helps confirm the accuracy of a resume and exposes those who have something negative to hide, such as a gap between jobs. And, these gaps could have been caused by a job he was fired from. If the human resource manager is the only person in the company willing to give a reference, then that is one of those darn old red flags. By the way, these red flags are usually on the attitude side. If you get too many red flags, you will need to watch out for charging bulls. Seriously, don't bother with human resource people unless someone transfers you to them before you can say, "Never mind."

With that stated, most applicants will have a list of about three references immediately available for you and some will have prepared lists of eight or more (the long lists usually have personal references which are useless). You should always make sure the applicant's previous supervisors are on the list. Ideally, one reference you want is a supervisor you know they worked for but not on their list. This is to ensure you're not working only from a list of admirers.

If managers have moved to different positions or jobs, you should track them down. Good applicants usually know how to contact them and are willing to assist you to find them.

Some applicants won't give their current employers as references if they haven't informed them of their intention to leave. In cases where the applicant has told her employer she intends to leave, the current supervisor is an excellent reference. (Legally, you must receive written approval first to talk to a current employer.) When he won't allow you to talk to a previous boss until hired, you can make the offer on the condition that there won't be any surprises with that reference.

Where to Call

Ninety percent of the time, you should call the reference at their office and ten percent at home. Calling a reference at home, if they don't mind or calling them at work, doesn't seem to make much difference.

Legal

Asking discriminating questions about the applicant is illegal. For example, don't ask about the candidates age, race, national origin, and so on. Again, it is also illegal to do a reference check on an applicant at his current company without his written approval. Any question that would be illegal to ask an applicant would also be illegal to ask a reference.

There is nothing wrong legally checking other people or agencies for information about the candidate, except you could go too far by going against the person's legal right to privacy. The wisest way to reduce that risk is to have the applicant sign a consent form at the end of the first interview before you start your checks. Remember, I am not an attorney, and you may want to check this out further.

How Many References Should be Called?
If the applicant is new to the workforce and has had little work history, three references contacted should be enough. Most mid-level applicants should be able to give you about four supervisor type references that you can contact. Contacting three supervisor references should be your minimum; six references may seem too many, but this is a case where more is better than less.

Get Specifics
References will be superficial with you if you allow them to. One of the reasons you interview an applicant before doing a reference check is to know enough about the applicant so that it is harder for the previous boss to exaggerate. For example, the previous boss says the applicant was a good administrator, even though your applicant was rationalizing doing XYZ reports late. You can ask, "But didn't you find he procrastinated on getting the XYZ reports to you? Why do you say he was a good administrator? What specifically did he do?" This will also establish yourself as an equal and not merely a clerk.

One of the questions on the reference interview form (at the end of this chapter), "What other strengths, assets and qualities did he/she have?" can bring out negatives. For example, if the previous employer is just warm on your person and gives minor praises, there are negatives in the closet for sure, especially if the person makes a big deal out of some minor aspect of the applicant, such as being great at following dress codes and arriving for work on time.

One of the most important questions is, "What would you consider her/his weaker points or areas needing improvement?" Often, references pause and then tell you they can't think of anything. Don't interrupt the pause. Wait and listen to what they tell you. If they do say, "Nothing," repeat your question like this, "We all have strengths and weaknesses. What were her/his weaknesses?" This is the point in the reference check that makes or breaks its value. Don't cave in.

The next most important questions are those about strengths and weaknesses you've already been alerted to in testing and interviewing. Start with the positive one and finish with the negative ones. Ask second and third questions to get as much clarity as possible. For example: You ask, "Our tests and interviewing showed she had a tendency to keep her ideas to herself. Did you notice that?" Reference says, "No, not really. I did notice she wouldn't tell you her concerns unless you directly asked her. Maybe that is what your tests showed." Now you have confirmation her assertiveness is low. You may try for a specific example, but then you may go over the edge with the reference and get nothing more.

Evaluation

Because employers are careful not to say anything bad about a former employee, they'll have a tendency to give you a good report on the applicant. Therefore, you need to notice very closely what and how the reference answers your questions. For example, a statement that the person could have worked harder is more likely to mean the person was very lazy.

Judge the candidates on the emotional responses the references give. For instance, when you ask the reference would she hire back the person again, and you get a pause and a less than enthusiastic "yes" you can note that as a bad indicator. On the other hand, it is a plus when a former employer speaks positively or enthusiastically about the applicant. If he is curt, brief, or relatively guarded, you should take that as a minus. The words spoken should only have secondary value.

If the responses are influenced by the previous employer's personality, that should also be taken into account. For example, a tyrannical type may sound grumpy about everything. You don't know this reference, but the fact he was negative about your call, your questions, and your candidate, means the words spoken have the most value.

If the former supervisors refuse to give you a reference and refer you to their human resources departments, you can take that as a minus, especially if several supervisors do this. Many former supervisors will tell you that their companies have policies about not giving references, but because the person was so good, they give a reference anyway. That is always a good sign.

Expectations

One of the major problems in the hiring process is the difference in expectations. This happens in reference checking as well as interviewing, for example, attempting to rate sales ability in interviewing. The candidate may brag about his ability to sell. The reference may say he was very good. Yet, when he comes to work for you, his production is average. This could be due to exaggeration, but it could also be due to levels of expectation. The applicant and the reference could have lower expectations of selling performance than you do. A good way around this situation is to ask references to compare the person to others. For example, "How did he compare to other salespeople you have or had?"

Education

If education is important to the position, you should check with the school. Education is rarely ever checked and dishonest candidates know it.

Prepare Your Questions in Advance

You should make up a form (see attached) with your questions and statements. Leave room for the answers. This form will enable you to be on top of the interview. The form also makes writing easier because you don't have to write the question down as well as the answer. In addition, the completed form serves as an important document to prove due diligence in case a negligent hiring suit occurs.

Fill in the applicant's name and the date you expect to do your reference checking, and fill in the areas you are concerned about in question thirteen. Also, cross off the "she" or "he" depending on the applicant's gender. Then photocopy the two pages for as many references as you expect to contact. This will save you a lot of time rewriting the same information.

Vendor Services

Some services do in-depth checking of public records. They will check into a person's criminal background, driving records, education, professional licenses, social security numbers, civil lawsuits involving candidates, and worker's compensation. Their fees range from approximately $300.00. If you want unbiased regular reference check, my company will do that for you.

Reference Check Interview Sheet

Reference's Name: _____

Phone: _____

Reference's position & company name: _____

Applicant's Name: _____

Date: _____

1. Thank them for returning or accepting your call.
2. Identify yourself, your position, your company.
3. Ask the reference if they have a few minutes to answer some questions about (applicant's name).
4. If you feel it's needed, reassure the reference that what you're told will be kept confidential, but you'll rarely need to do this.
5. Describe the position the applicant is applying for.
6. How do you think he/she might fit in that position? (*Get specifics.*)
7. What did she/he do for you?
8. How well did he/she do it?
9. How would you compare him to others doing a similar job?
10. Would you rehire (or work for) the person again?
11. What other strengths, assets, and qualities did she/he have?

   Note: *It's okay to interrupt in this question to get more specifics.*

12. What were his/her weaker points, or areas needing improvement?

   Note: *Don't interrupt in this question because the reference may become cautious and end too quickly. Keep asking for more weak points until the reference says he can't think of any more. Then ask questions about the answers.*

13. I had a sense during the interview that the applicant was a little:
    a. moody
    b. unorganized
    c. impatient
    d. defensive
    e. meek
    f. critical
    g. arrogant
    h. opinionated
    i. stubborn
    j. _____ *(Add traits you may be concerned about.)*
    k. _____
    l. _____
14. How does she/he react when things go wrong?
15. From one to ten, how well did he/she get along with coworkers? From one to ten with management?
16. How would you rate his/her attendance?
17. What is the best way to supervise her/him?
18. Why do you think he/she is interested in this position?
19. Ask the following from the application form if this information hasn't already come up.
    a) Employment dates: (from) _____ (to) _____
    b) Pay: _____
    c) Job title: _____
20. Do you have any final comments or suggestions about her/him?
21. Interviewer's comments. *(Do this right after the interview.)*
22. You may want to prioritize these questions in case the reference doesn't have time to answer them all. Don't forget to thank them for their time.

Chapter 13

Legal Issues

The purpose of this book is to hire talented team players. In order to do this, you will turn down many people who think their skills and experience alone should get them the job. For example, a wolf, by their very nature of causing problems, is far more likely to get into a lawsuit than a good-natured person. Therefore, you will be stronger knowing the best legal way to avoid future problems. Scan through the following and look for hazy areas or subjects to focus on.

Never have so many candidates known their legal rights so well, causing so much grief to employers. And they are willing to fight you over them. A qualified wolf candidate with an obvious disability, for example, could get you into a world of problems. Instead of causing problems when they work for you, they can now do it when you turn them down.

A dollar saved is a dollar made. Based on this concept, you can make a lot of money reading this chapter, especially if you have never studied labor laws.

I did a lot of legal research on the unique subjects I address in this book: interviewing, testing, assessing attitudes, and assessing personalities. Most of what I write in this chapter is taken almost directly from a book or other document written by an attorney. However, I am not an attorney; I haven't even spent one day in law school; the one college law course I did hardly qualifies me as an attorney. The information in this chapter may help raise your awareness of possible legal pitfalls, but legal advice should be gained from professional sources.

Just to be perfectly clear. This chapter is designed to provide accurate and authoritative information about the subject matter covered. It is a summary but if legal advice is required, the services of a competent attorney should be sought. In other words, don't hang on my every word. Use what I say as a guide to do your own research.

The following are some of the areas to watch out for in the hiring process. If you have any concerns about these areas, contact a good labor attorney, the state's Fair Employment Department, or the Federal Equal Employment Opportunity Commission (EEOC). You can also find good legal hiring books at the local library.

Discrimination

You can cause yourself legal problems in the following ways:

* Making a decision not to hire someone based on discriminatory reasons.
* Asking certain discriminatory questions.
* Using certain discriminatory screening practices.

I compiled the following illegal, discriminatory questions from a government brochure and books written by attorneys:

* Age/Date of Birth. Dates of attendance or completion of elementary or high school. Questions that tend to identify applicants over age forty.
* Arrest? (Different from convictions, see convictions below.)
* Religion or religious days observed? Available for Saturday or Sunday work? (Legally the employer can state regular days, hours or shifts to be worked.)
* Children under eighteen?

* Number of children?
* Age of children?
* What arrangements for care of minor children?
* Citizenship? Place of birth of applicant? Parents? Spouse or relatives?
* Green card before employment. (You can ask, "After employment, can you submit verification of your legal right to work in the U.S.?")
* Convictions (other than traffic)? You can only ask this type of question if the question is accompanied by a statement from you saying that a conviction won't necessarily disqualify the applicant from employment.
* Credit record? (Except under special circumstances involving the handling of money. Check with your state for more specifics)
* Traffic violations inquires and requests for Motor Vehicle records are ok for jobs that require driving but not for those that do not.
* Eye, skin, and hair color?
* Fidelity bond ever refused?
* Friends or relations working for us?
* Height? Weight?
* Photographs affixed to an application.
* Lowest salary acceptable?
* Organizations, clubs, societies, and lodges? (It is acceptable to list job-related ones, and omit those that indicate race, religious creed, color, national origin, ancestry, gender or age.)
* Maiden name?
* House mates? (Don't ask with whom you reside, or do you live with your parents?)
* Mother's tongue or language you commonly use?
* Marital status?
* Mr., Miss, Mrs., or Ms?
* Prior married name?
* Current or past assets, liabilities or credit rating, including bankruptcy or garnishment?
* Sexual preferences?

* Gender?
* Spouse's name?
* Spouse's work?
* Widowed, divorced, or separated?
* Physical limitations or conditions? Medical condition? (Cancer, for example). (See section on The American's with Disabilities Act following this section.)
* Own or rent home?
* Pregnancy, childbearing or birth control?
* Military services, dates and types of discharge?

The federal law behind the discrimination requirements is the 1964 Civil Rights Act, Title VI and VII, covering discrimination based on race, color, national origin, gender (including sexual harassment), and religion.

The employment discrimination laws favor the employee applicant. All the applicant has to do is prove a surface level of discrimination and the burden of proof moves to the employer. This surface-level proof is called *prima facie*, which means "on the face of it." One way an applicant can show *prima facie* evidence is to show that the employer has an imbalance of women or minorities of current employees compared to who's available in the workforce. Proving he didn't discriminate can be difficult, expensive and time-consuming for the employer.

What to do When a Candidate Volunteers Discriminatory Information

Listening to a candidate tell you discriminatory information is perfectly legal. For example, if candidates tell you they have a spouse and children, you don't legally have to stop them from telling you. The following are three actions you should never take:

* Never write the information down.
* Never inquire further about it.
* Never pass the information to another.

Take Advantage of the Americans with Disabilities Act (ADA)

What is the Americans with Disabilities Act (ADA)? It is a federal law that requires you to provide a reasonable accommodation to a qualified person with a disability, unless it would create an undue hardship for your business. ADA seeks to make sure a person isn't excluded from a job simply because she can't perform some marginal duties listed in a job description. For example, an outgoing person with a good attitude applies for a receptionist job, but has an artificial arm and can only type with one hand. You want someone who can type about 30 minutes a day between phone calls. Because the typing part is considered a "marginal" duty, you legally cannot reject her for her inability to type rapidly. On the other hand, because it may be difficult for her to find a job and because she may be so thankful to have the job, she just may be the best receptionist you ever had, as well as averting the possibility of a lawsuit.

The Americans with Disabilities Act prohibits any pre-employment questions about disabilities. To avoid legal problems, focus on the candidate's ability to perform the job, not on the disability. For example, after describing the job, ask, "Are you able to perform this work with or without some sort of modification on our part?" If he or she says "Yes" then you can ask, "How would you perform the job with these changes?"

If you are a Human Resource Manager, you know about these requirements. I won't get into them in detail because this is not the purpose of this book. At this point, you may be wondering what you need to do to keep out of legal trouble. My suggestion is to take any doubtful disability questions to the Human Resource manager because follow up interviews with a disabled person can get complicated.

The next question may be how to keep out of legal trouble if someone sits down in front of you and is missing a hand, leg, eye, deaf, talks with a lisp, or complains of depression. The first answer is whatever you do—don't (as in never) ask about the disability. Don't even ask if it seems like a good conversational topic. Conduct your interview like you would with someone who does not have such disabilities. After the interview, go to your Human Resource manager to find out what to do next.

The only other question is what legally makes up a disability. The answer is anything that prevents a person from doing any of the following:

* Walking
* Speaking
* Breathing
* Performing manual tasks
* Seeing
* Hearing
* Learning
* Taking care of oneself
* Working
* Sitting
* Standing
* Lifting
* Reading

Therefore, because of ADA, you are not allowed to ask orally or in writing any of the following:

* Diseases and illnesses. For example, don't ask, "Have you ever been treated for high blood pressure?"
* Hospitalization.
* Treatment from a psychologist or psychiatrist.
* Treatment for a mental condition.
* Health related reasons people may not be able to perform a job? For example, don't ask, "Is there any health-related reason you may not be able to drive this van and make deliveries?"
* Attendance due to illness. For example, don't ask, "How many days did you miss last year, from work, because of an illness?"
* Prescribed or illegal drugs. For example, don't ask, "What medications do you take?"

* Treatment the person has had for drug or alcohol addiction.
* Workers compensation filings.

Appearance

You can turn down people based on their appearance if it's job-related. For example, a cosmetic company can require their salespeople to have healthy-looking skin, but they can't legally require that from their accounts people who don't interact face-to-face with the public.

Reference Checks

The legal purpose for investigating an applicant's background is to make sure the person will do a good job for you and fit in with other employees. However, you can overdo it invading a person's privacy. Calling an applicant's current employer for a reference, without specific approval, is one of the worst invasions. Even calling others without written approval is risky. And, if it is appropriate to do credit checks, because the people will be handling large sums of money, you should get specific written approval first.

A good way to reduce most of the risk is to have the person sign a written approval for you to check into their past. The wording should allow the interviewing company to obtain information from previous employers, schools, or any other applicable places. A good place for this is on the application form. Remember, credit checks and current employers will need specific approvals.

When you do talk to previous employers or acquaintances, do not ask them about the applicant's race, color, religious creed, national origin, ancestry, physical handicap, medical condition, marital status, gender, age, or sexual orientation.

Due Diligence in Investigating the Applicant

You can also get into legal trouble for not checking into people. Hiring a criminal without taking sufficient steps to investigate the person and not documenting that you did so is an example. The problem would occur when the criminal acts against another employee or customer, and that employee or customer sues you for negligent hiring. For instance, you unknowingly hire a guy who has a criminal record for robbery, and he steels another employee's purse.

Testing

Skill, aptitude, honesty, and attitude testing are valuable tools to assist in finding the right applicants but if you do it carelessly, it can be a legal liability. If you intend to use medical testing (this includes testing for depression), drug testing, or polygraph testing you should consult an attorney for your state.

Personality, honesty, and attitude testing are legal if the questions are not discriminatory. For example of two illegal questions, "Are you attracted to members of the opposite sex?" or "Are you a Christian?" In addition, questions about disabilities are also illegal. For example, "Are you currently seeing a psychologist or psychiatrist?" Therefore, it is important to make sure the questions on the questionnaires you intend to use are legal.

Skill tests are illegal if they don't measure the important aspects of the job. Employers could have a tough time defending discrimination attacks if the tests measure skills not related to the job opening. Specifically, you can get into trouble if she failed the test and that was the reason for turning her down. For example, you give an Asian truck driver a sales test and you then tell him he was not considered because he failed the test. You would have the problem of proving why you were using a non-related test to turn down a minority and not using the test on the ones you hired.

Testing becomes a problem when it tends to screen out applicants without using other forms of inquiry, such as interviews. If you use legal testing questions to obtain information that you further investigate, it's unlikely you will have a legal problem. You should carefully study the following paragraphs if you intend to screen applicants out using test results only.

Obviously, using a test that openly discriminates is going to cause problems, but so will more subtle versions. For example, using a test that you think will improve the workforce but in reality does not could be hard to defend. Unintentional discrimination is not a legally accepted excuse.

You need to prove to yourself that you could defend a skill test as being relevant and correct. This is called validating a test. The following are some of the aspects that must be present:

* Existing employees must score well on the skill test. Performance and test scores must match.
* When testing existing employees, you must take into account the training they've had in the company, as well as how the existing people measured when they first started with the company.
* A skill test must measure a quality that can't be easily learned. For example, a skill in running a copy machine that can be learned in a few hours would not be a valid skill to test.
* The skill test can measure the relevant jobs the employer expects the applicant to grow into in a reasonable period. Some government guidelines define "a reasonable period of time" as less than five years.
* The skill tests must be understandable to minorities with a different native language.
* The result of testing shouldn't cause a lack of women or minorities in the workforce.

If the test you are using is not validated by yourself, it can still be used. In this case, you should use the results for research and clues for what to look for in interviews and reference checking. To be safe, you may want to use a cover letter on the test, stating the results of the test won't be used to make a hiring decision. Validation can be done by checking the tested people you did hire and seeing how they performed. In addition, you should have tests available in other languages for those who request them.

You can't rely solely on screening candidates by officially validated tests until you have also validated them for the particular job position in your company. In sales for instance, the job can be very different from one company to the next.

Once you have a validated test, you should set a standard that is not too high. One judge made the comment that "Tests are not to become masters of reality."

If employers are sued for discriminating based on test results only and they can't show obvious proof of test validity, they are left with two weak defenses:

* The business necessity of its action, which mean the tests help the business be more efficient.
* A "bona fide occupational qualification," which means the need to be productive in a certain way.

In my research, I found government encouragement for the use of tests. I also found no legal or government opinion that says minorities should be given preferential treatment – only equal treatment.

If you want to read more on this subject of testing, go to the county law library, which is free and open to the public. Read the testing guidelines under "Code of Federal Regulations" 29 part 1607 and two landmark decisions by the *U.S. Supreme Court Griggs v. Duke Power Co. 1971*, and *Albermarle Paper Co. V. Moody 1975*, and other relevant cases.

You can also contact the state's Fair Employment Department or the federal Equal Employment Opportunity Commission (EEOC) for more information. They are there to enforce the hiring laws. They also act as mediators to resolve disputes between applicants and employers.

In addition, the same test discrimination laws apply to interview questions, interview forms, tests for internal promotions, and transfers.

If you do decide to use written tests, only give them to people who are applying for jobs that require reading. This is because the inability to read is a disability. For example, a heavy equipment driver doesn't get the job because he couldn't read the assessment questions properly, and the results falsely indicated an attitude problem. My assessments measure ability to read and they also measures inconsistencies. When the applicant does poorly on the reading part of my assessments, which occurs about one in one hundred, you legally need to read the questions to the applicant and in some cases explain the questions. Do this unless the ability to read is an important part of the job.

The ability to read for a heavy equipment driver position is considered a "marginal requirement" (see ADA already covered in this chapter) and should not be used to turn the applicant down. In some cases, it is important the driver can read and in these situations it is possible to use the person's inability to read as a reason to turn him down.

If you give the test to one driver, you must give it to all that you are seriously considering.

In the twenty-three years I've been consulting business leaders, I've never heard of anyone having legal problems with testing. This is not to say attorneys haven't heard about such problems. Don't be afraid to use tests, just make sure you do it in a legal way.

Who Can You Legally Not Hire?

You are legally free to reject those who lack the necessary skills and experience. Those who can't perform or who aren't reliable can also be turned down. You can cast aside anyone based on factors that are logically tied to a valid business purpose.

How to Turn Applicants Down

The best way to turn down an applicant is to inform them you're no longer considering them for the position. Don't give them a specific reason, no matter how much they beg you for it. Say they have some great qualities (most people do); unfortunately, they don't fit the profile you're looking for.

More Recent Insights

It is important to defend your company if any claims are ever made. This means not settling unless you are sure that your company was in the wrong. Frivolous claims are on the rise and local EEOC boards are aware of this.

That means the tables are turning in favor of the employer to some degree. If you have a valid legal reason for terminating or not hiring someone you can easily defend yourself and win. It takes some effort but reduced unemployment insurance costs add up. More importantly once you settle, the attorneys who represent these frivolous cases smell blood and come for more. Take advantage of relationships you have with your insurance companies and your own resources to defend your rights as an equal opportunity employer.

It's Not That Serious

If you made it through all those details, I congratulate you for a study well done. I always think about something an attorney once told me: "We see all the problems and very few successes. Therefore we warn our clients about things that are unlikely to happen." I am not an attorney, so to me I never hear of legal hiring problems, even though I know most managers break the hiring laws. Despite that, you never know when someone will take advantage of those negligent managers.

Many of those involved in hiring will need to change their faulty and illegal ways of interviewing to be able to find super team players. For example, asking about a person's family, which is illegal and mostly ineffective, takes away from effective interviewing. If the manager stops asking illegal questions, he will have to replace those questions with more effective and legal ones. If you try the interview procedure in Chapter Eleven, you will not only be more effective, but more legal and less likely to get sued.

If the idea of pre-employment testing is interesting to you, the next chapter is for you.

Chapter 14

Testing

If you don't test applicants, what do you have to rely on? A resume that is a list of exaggerated positives that conveniently leaves out any negatives. You have the candidate's verbal answers to your questions which are a further extension of the resume. And you see the way the person physically looks and acts plus your own intuition. You even notice the person's physical presence and actions then they are in their best behavior mode. Finally, if you can interview flawlessly, it will still take about six hours of interviewing to cover all the twelve queries on a mid-level position.

Just to be clear, the tests I'm referring to are designed to aid an employer's search for a suitable employee. Some tests are written personality and attitude assessments while others are timed problem solving tests. You also have practical hands on testing, such as typing and drug tests.

The Downside of Testing
Just like anything else, some business leaders think testing is a necessity, and some have negative ideas about it. This is understandable because testing is far from a perfect science. Some people even think testing is illegal. What is the truth?

From a legal standpoint, testing is like interviewing. It is legal in the United States if it is not used to discriminate. (See the previous chapter on legal issues.) How do you use a test to discriminate? The employer decides she doesn't want someone because she doesn't like the skin color. For instance, the employer gives a guy, applying for a typist position, a math test. When he fails, the employer can say he was not good enough. That example is obvious, but what about an employer who thinks a certain race is no good. That employer may not realize her testing program is designed to fail all those types.

The Value of Testing

Because I test people for a living, my poor associates get used as guinea pigs. On one occasion, Paul Louie did a full set of tests and I noticed the "Ability to Read" result was awful. Yet, he had graduated from college. When I asked him about that, he told me how he had used that disability to change requirements so he could graduate. Then one day he was desperate for a job, which motivated him to apply for an administrative assistant position. When he got the job, I remember thinking, "That poor business owner doesn't know the problem she hired." And sure enough, a few months and a pile of frustration later Paul got his walking papers. One little test would have saved a lot of misery for both of them.

In my day-to-day business environment, I see many of the test results before and after people get hired. A high percentage of applicants are just like Paul, applying for jobs they have no business going after. When the employers get impatient and hire people the tests indicate they shouldn't, they all regret it later. The employers who test and interview, and hold out for those who fit the profile, make it a point to tell me how great the person turned out in reality.

Those who think tests are valuable feel that test results open their eyes to what may never have been apparent from interviewing or reference checking. A common example, a candidate may look assertive in the interview, but the tests show a different story. If the position was for sales that required assertiveness, and the person didn't have it, there would be a problem in low sales. Those who have found value in testing usually experiment with different types of tests and continue using the best.

I remember a client who was having a problem with one of his engineers because she didn't document her work well and produced little for the time spent on projects. My client couldn't understand this as they had been friends for years, and this engineer had lots of experience as an engineer. We tested her and found out she had little interest in doing detail, documentation, and organization, all of which is important to engineering. Engineers should enjoy and feel comfortable doing detail work. In other words, these people should have an analyzer/logical personality. This particular engineer was expressive/social (see Chapter Three), which is opposite to the ideal engineer. That explained why my client was having a problem. Unfortunately, many people go into professions that aren't suited to their personalities. If you test before hiring, you'll reduce your chances of making such mistakes.

Testing often exposes the extent of a bad trait. For example, in the interview you may get hints that the person is too critical, but the test results will show if it is a concern or not. This saves time in interviewing, but more importantly increases your effectiveness.

Testing also allows you to see the larger picture of a candidate. Thus, it often reveals aspects of the candidate you may not have thought about asking. For instance, if the candidate scored poorly on the ability to read test, this could lead you to question the person's ability to write. This may be important for the position offered. Verbal interviews alone wouldn't have detected such a weakness.

Another benefit of testing is to help in the decision making process between two good finalists. Although this is far less of an issue when you're following the ideas in this book, it can happen. I remember having two great candidates for one position. In every way they seemed equal, but the test results revealed relevant weaknesses in one of the candidates and the decision was easy.

Another important benefit of testing is the time you save as a manager. Tests will narrow down the areas of concern in a candidate's personality and the areas of no concern. The manager is then able to focus in on the areas that indicated concern and determine if those areas will be manageable. Before an interview assignment, look over test results and plan your focus of questions. In a short time, you will have an accurate idea of the true value of the candidate.

The Different Tests

I have found the following tests to be the most valuable. They are listed in order of importance.

Personality or Aptitude Tests: These tests are usually 50 to 500 multiple-choice questions in length or contain lists of words to choose from. The best test results will show personality traits and a personality type, such as an Analyzer/Logical. For example, my personality assessment examines twenty-one different traits and four basic personality styles. It reveals if the candidate will match the personality requirement for a position. It also gives you traits to explore in interviewing and reference checking. Providing the candidates can read the questions, these tests work well on people who work with their hands, their minds, their communication skills or any other type of skill.

In order to assure complete accuracy in personality assessments, they should have a built-in honesty check to detect if, and when, applicants are exaggerating or covering up weaker traits. Most of these tests have this check, but some don't. I strongly recommend using only those tests that have this safeguard; otherwise, the candidate's assessment results may be exaggerated. For example, a weak candidate trying to get a job by exaggeration may look good.

Attitude Tests: These assessments are often called opinion surveys or honesty tests. They give lists of true or false opinions for candidates to select. These assessments work best on people who can read and who are qualified for jobs that require the use of their minds more than their hands. Therefore, these types of assessments should have a short reading test associated with them.

From my experience in developing these types of assessments, it takes considerable research to ensure accuracy. This is because people applying for a job usually select different answers than those who have a job. I think it has to do with applicants trying to make a good impression, as opposed to those who feel confident they won't lose their jobs. Because the research on candidates can only be done on those applying for jobs and because people can fake a good attitude for many months, it takes about a year to validate accuracy of the attitude tests. In my 20 years of research, true improvements have only been possible examining the way candidates filled in these types of questionnaires and how they turned out in reality from the supervisor's point of view one year later.

Due to the importance of attitude in hiring, I strongly recommend you use a reliable attitude test for anyone applying for a job.

Competency Tests: Many people think that analytical IQ results measure competency. Many of the current testing companies cater to this public demand by selling analytical IQ tests to hiring managers. But from my experience during the early to mid-1990s, I found little correlation between competent employees and incompetent ones and their IQ results when they applied for a job. However, I did find emotional intelligence played a major factor in the competence or incompetence of employees. Emotional competence has to do with ability to focus, stay motivated, communicate, and have self-confidence.

The Following Tests Can be Used if the Prior Tests were Positive

Hands on Tests: These tests involve having the applicant do certain specified tasks while the tester watches. For example, have the applicant operate computer software programs while watching on and looking for proficiency. Other examples may include jobs requiring physical activities like handling tools and equipment.

Detail Tests: These tests give many samples of minor mistakes which the person must discover and note. The answers are graded on accuracy and speed. Give them to accountants, programmers, administrative assistants, and others who need to be accurate with details. Don't give it to people who don't need to be good at detail, such as sales people selling simple products.

Detail tests measure the *ability* to do detail, rather than the *interest* in doing detail. These are two different subjects. Many people are good with details but don't like to mess with them. Therefore, the profile of a detail-type sales job would require the ability to accurately do detail, but not necessarily the interest in doing it. This is the reason sales people are notorious for not doing written reports. Wimbush has a test like this which is supplied as a free addition to the WIMBUSH-IC and WIMBUSH-SL tests.

Math tests: These tests are used to measure a candidate's ability to do accounting work. Wimbush has a test like this which is supplied as an addition to the WIMBUSH-IC and WIMBUSH-SL tests.

Problem Solving Tests: These are also known as IQ tests. They list problems that the applicant must solve within a set period of time. The number of correct answers determines the level of intelligence. Give these tests to engineers and others who need problem solving skills to succeed. I've found, for example, that good salespeople don't always do well on intelligence tests. As most people know by now, IQ test results have limited general value, but if you use them on people solving mental and theoretical problems, they can be valuable. Notice I put it close to the bottom, as it has the lowest importance.

Drug Tests: Because the cheapest way of testing drug use is through urinalysis, this is the most common drug test. However, the error rate from urinalysis is between five and fifteen percent. If you do decide to use drug testing, I would strongly advise getting legal advice before proceeding.

Making the Decision

Deciding what and how to use tests requires some thought. However, when you figure out your program, you will only need to check its value from time to time. The time saved and the better quality people you hire will pay for the up-front time invested approximately ten times over.

Chapter 15

Improving Your Competence In Hiring

To be good at hiring talented team players will require many skills and the interest to learn them. To still be reading this book tells me you have the interest to learn what it will take. Every chapter describes one or more skills and the good news is that all you can learn these skills. With study and restudy of each chapter, and if you review people you hired, you will end up consistently hiring great people.

Revisit the People You Hired

How could you be expected to learn how to play golf, or any sport for that matter, if you are never allowed to see what happens to your ball? All you are told is your score at the end of the game. Even a good golfer would cringe at that. Yet that is how most people hire. They never know how effective their questions were or how accurate their opinions were when they did the interview. In the present, all they know is how the person turned out: bad, Okay, or good.

One of the best ways to get that vital feedback is to take notes of what candidates say and what you thought during the interview. Then you should revisit the files of those you were involved in hiring after their honeymoon period is over. Carefully read through the files to see how accurate your predictions were. Start with your pros and cons list on the candidate. This of course is another good reason to write down your pros and cons. If you're familiar with the person, note where you were correct and where you were wrong. If you are not familiar with the person, check with their supervisor for more specific input. Then look through your interview notes to discover how you chose the pros and cons. Also, look at the test results as you do this. Start making mental adjustments of what you could have done better. Restudy the applicable chapters in this book where you suspect you went wrong. You will find this exercise an important educational tool because you will learn what corrective actions to take on yourself.

Revisit Testing Results

If you have done any testing, you can see how to better interpret the results you get. It will help you understand how different types of people respond to tests. It will give a better feel for what traits are significant or not. For example, a test result may show a person who is too critical and blames too much, and now you realize this is the reason why you terminated him. In the future, you will watch for this more closely and make better hiring decisions. After a while, you will understand how they may or may not predict future competence and attitude. Then you can start relying on testing for better hiring decisions.

Over the years, I have read many books on hiring and interviewing. Although this has been useful in many ways, I got my real education following up on people I have interviewed. This activity put all the theory into perspective.

Practice Asking Questions

Many people and business leaders fall into the same trap. They are not good listeners and do not know how to ask good questions, they focus on telling and doing. Interviewing takes careful listening and great questions. Many hiring managers do not practice these skills for several reasons, the two most common reasons are lack of awareness or they do not practice. After reading this book you should be fully aware of how to interview effectively, now all you need to do is practice regularly. Hopefully, you are not experiencing high levels of turn over creating many opportunities to practice. If you are like most business leaders you will need to find other avenues to refine your craft. The easiest way to do this is practice asking your current employees really good questions all the time. Instead of telling people things practice asking questions that lead them to answers or uncover misunderstanding. First you will discover when your employees don't understand a key concept and secondarily you will reinforce their good thoughts. You will learn to think of good questions and listen for the underlining meaning in their answers. This will make you a better interviewer.

The New Way of Hiring

The old traditional way of looking for top producers, with a good educational background, and who come across well in interviews tended to fill companies with many negative people. This new way of thinking about hiring people who will culturally fit into the organization, have a good attitude, and show a genuine interest in the position, will need to be learned. Don't be surprised if the difference between the traditional organization and the future organization is night and day.

From another viewpoint, our whole society is moving toward greater sensitivity and demand for self-esteem and self-awareness. Our society uses the term self-esteem more and more often. A few years ago, even the State government of California was supporting self-esteem. If you are not hiring managers, executives, and leaders who are supportive of self-esteem and self-awareness, your company runs the risk of being left behind. Therefore, hiring for more than just skills, education, and competence is another way of leading your business into a new progressive era.

The goal of hiring is to find people who will be productive in their assigned positions while contributing to the team spirit of the organization. The trick is to find people capable of producing well, contributing to the team spirit of the organization, and staying for the long haul. To be able to do this in a high percentage of hires is a valuable skill which you can learn from this book.

About the Author

Kingsley Wimbush has consulted hundreds of business leaders for the last 25 years. When he first started on this adventure, he thought it was just a matter of passing on good ideas. However, after eight years of this endeavor, he was thoroughly disillusioned. Around Eighteen years ago, he realized that most of his business clients were more concerned about negative, uncaring, and troublesome employees than good ideas. After spending a couple of years trying to help them with those uncooperative individuals, he decided it was also a good idea to help them hire good people in the first place. Kingsley even designed a set of assessments to ensure they were hiring good people. He also helped train them and their managers to make better hiring decisions by teaching them how to spot good candidates, evaluate resumes, interview, and do reference checks. Kingsley wrote many papers about hiring for his clients in the early 1990's and condensed them into a hiring manual in 1994.

Kingsley also has a pre-employment assessment service he developed over the last 20 years. When results of important applicants were borderline, his clients would ask him to interview them and do reference checks on them. A researcher by nature, Kingsley would also check how these candidates turned out in reality and traced back which interview questions helped the most and included them in this manual.

Through his clients, he has heard almost everything good and bad that can happen in the hiring process. From this feedback, he upgraded the manual several times. Finally, the minor upgrades where not enough, so he rewrote this manual to include everything important he knew about hiring great team players and to point out the current changes in our culture.

Today, Kingsley's assessments are used around the world and business leaders validate the results by using them year after year. He coaches many hiring managers one-on-one, helps design hiring procedures and gives workshops for those involved.

Kingsley has also written a high volume of other manuals, procedures and papers on business techniques.

His son has followed in his footsteps. Since his passing Fletcher has successfully filled his role in coaching business leaders on hiring practices that produce results. Fletcher is looking forward to publishing more books on hiring and management in the future.

www.ingramcontent.com/pod-product-compliance
Lightning Source LLC
Chambersburg PA
CBHW070234190526
45169CB00001B/185